T0063865

To:

_____

From:

_____

Date:

_____

WENDI LOU LEE

Baby Grace on *Little House on the Prairie*

A PRAIRIE DEVOTIONAL

INSPIRED BY THE BELOVED TV SERIES

THOMAS NELSON

Since 1798

A Prairie Devotional

© 2019 Wendi Lou Lee

Published in Nashville, Tennessee, by Thomas Nelson. Thomas Nelson is a registered trademark of HarperCollins Christian Publishing, Inc.

Scripture quotations marked CEV are from the Contemporary English Version. Copyright © 1991, 1992, 1995 by American Bible Society. Used by permission. Scripture quotations marked ESV are from the ESV® Bible (The Holy Bible, English Standard Version®). Copyright © 2001 by Crossway, a publishing ministry of Good News Publishers. Used by permission. All rights reserved. Scripture quotations marked KJV are from the King James Version. Public domain. Scripture quotations marked MSG are from *The Message*. Copyright © 1993, 2002, 2018 by Eugene H. Peterson. Used by permission of NavPress. All rights reserved. Represented by Tyndale House Publishers, Inc. Scripture quotations marked NASB are from New American Standard Bible®. Copyright © 1960, 1962, 1963, 1968, 1971, 1972, 1973, 1975, 1977, 1995 by The Lockman Foundation. Used by permission. www.Lockman.org Scripture quotations marked NIV are from the Holy Bible, New International Version®, NIV®. Copyright © 1973, 1978, 1984, 2011 by Biblica, Inc.™ Used by permission of Zondervan. All rights reserved worldwide. www.Zondervan.com. The "NIV" and "New International Version" are trademarks registered in the United States Patent and Trademark Office by Biblica, Inc.® Scripture quotations marked NLT are from the Holy Bible, New Living Translation. © 1996, 2004, 2015 by Tyndale House Foundation. Used by permission of Tyndale House Ministries, Carol Stream, Illinois 60188. All rights reserved. Scripture quotations marked NLV are from the New Life Version. © Christian Literature International. Scripture quotations marked NRSV are from New Revised Standard Version Bible. Copyright © 1989 National Council of the Churches of Christ in the United States of America. Used by permission worldwide. All rights reserved. Scripture quotations marked TLB are from The Living Bible. Copyright © 1971. Used by permission of Tyndale House Publishers a Division of Tyndale House Ministries, Carol Stream, Illinois 60188. All rights reserved. Scripture quotations marked TPT are from The Passion Translation®. Copyright © 2017, 2018 by Passion & Fire Ministries, Inc. Used by permission. All rights reserved. ThePassionTranslation.com.

ISBN 978-1-4002-1328-3 (audiobook)
ISBN 978-1-4002-1327-6 (eBook)
ISBN 978-1-4002-4725-7 (SC)

In memory of Laura Ingalls Wilder—
for the stories she told
and her faith in God.

WELCOME TO MY
LITTLE HOUSE

My family's favorite gathering place is the hand-me-down couch filled with colorful pillows in our living room, a brimming bookcase along one side, and a white-mantled fireplace on the other. On the top shelf of the corner hutch sits a framed photo of my twin sister, Brenda, and me. We are snuggled on Michael Landon's lap.

"Pa" is playfully grinning as though he's the luckiest man on earth.

Whenever I look at that photo, I grin too. At eight months old, Brenda and I were cast as Baby Grace, Charles Ingalls's youngest daughter, for the television series *Little House on the Prairie*. The four seasons we spent as Baby Grace turned our lives right-side-up. Although too young to grasp our good fortune, we have since come to realize that we were—are—the lucky ones, blessed to have been part of a television family that modeled for us what a real family can be.

I don't know if your parents watched *Little House* with you the way mine did, but it was a tradition I carried on when I became a parent. When my daughter began kindergarten, the Ingalls family entertained us every Monday night. With each episode, I gleaned nuggets of wisdom from Charles and Caroline, and even from the unlikely character of Nellie Oleson.

Many of the relationship and faith connections I had missed when watching as a child now jumped out at me as an adult. I saw relevant lessons for today, and the episodes became opportunities for family discussions.

One night, as all of us crowded onto the couch watching a favorite *Little House* episode, my husband suggested that I write a devotional built on the show's themes. Although it sounded like a great idea, I didn't have the confidence to try. Growing up in a broken home and being the younger twin, I struggled with self-doubt. A devotional sounded like a task too great for me to attempt.

Years of joy and heartache went by, both for our family and for the Ingallses. As we watched the Ingalls family overcome challenges week after week, I noticed how universal and timeless the themes were. We all struggle with loneliness, illness, setbacks, and loss. I had been diagnosed with a brain tumor and was dealing with insecurity, grief, and the unknowns of brain surgery. My family's challenges were no different from those of the Ingalls family. Just as *Little House* encouraged us, I could encourage others—if I paid heed to Pa, that is. "All you can do is try," he'd said.

This devotional is the result of doing just that.

First airing in 1974 and running for nine seasons, the television series was based on Laura Ingalls Wilder's children's books. Wilder charmed the world with her delightful stories of growing up as a pioneer girl. Although her stories are not all happy, they do encourage and inspire. Underlying her adventures is a strong faith in a good God, faith to which the television series stayed true.

Within these pages are stories of joy and heartache, fear and triumph, doubt and strength, each story a testament of faith that helped the Ingalls family—and our family—navigate life's challenges. I invite you to gather your family on your couch and join me as we step into the world of the Ingallses and into a closer walk with God.

Wendi Lou Lee

I

BECOME A STORYTELLER

"You better get some more paper then. Your grandpa's
got a whole lifetime of stories in his head."
—CAROLINE INGALLS

How we live our lives determines what kind of story we can tell. Every day we choose to dive deep into life or watch it pass by. We can live an epic life without visiting exotic places or having extravagant experiences; we just need to engage in the epic-ness of our own backyards and anywhere our feet might tread. When we live with this attitude, stories emerge, stories we can't help but share.

When Caroline's mother passes away, her grieving father loses the will to live. He resolves to wait passively and watch his life end—until Albert asks about his childhood. A story erupts from his brittle soul, and he becomes a passionate storyteller of his past.

Like Grandpa Holbrook, my grandmother lost her spouse after forty-seven years of marriage. Grandma Lou was a storyteller when we were growing up. I remember the famous childhood tale of life on her family farm in Minnesota, hunting down a chicken with an axe—and then her expression when she told us how the headless chicken chased her around the barnyard. She said killing Sunday dinner was the worst of all chores. I must have heard that story a hundred times.

After my grandfather died, Grandma Lou kept right on living. Her adventures and memories only became more epic, not because the experiences were grand, but because every day captivated her.

Every visit became a spillway of new stories, moments when she chose to fully live. The opportunities she embraced were transformed into more exciting encounters to share with us. I encourage you to experience and share the extraordinary life God's given you.

What kind of story are you living? Is it a life worth retelling? Take the plunge. Don't spectate; participate, and then share what happens. When Grandpa Holbrook started telling stories, he was inspired to keep living. Writing his memoir gave him a bounce in his step and a sparkle in his eyes. All it took was one story to breathe new life into him.

Live your life in a way that your stories will be told a hundred times over.

Tell your children about it in the years to come, and let your children tell their children. Pass the story down from generation to generation.

JOEL 1:3 NLT

Are you more likely to experience the day and see it as an adventure or sit and watch from the sidelines? How can you engage in the opportunities God puts in front of you?

2

FATEFUL LUNCH DATE

"Things are meant to be."
—SAM SHELBY

I believe God has a plan, an intention from the beginning. He puts us in exactly the right places at the right times to accomplish His will. God used Sam Shelby, a blind man, to save Charles on a hunting trip. Sam had given up on being useful until Laura came running for help. Helping was his destiny.

My role as Baby Grace was God's idea. My sister and I weren't infants pursuing a career, and my mother never dreamed of being an acting manager. It happened by the grace of God.

My grandmother was a friend of Sue McCray, the casting director for *Little House on the Prairie*. They were chatting over lunch when Sue revealed that she couldn't find twins to portray Charles Ingalls's youngest daughter. We were exactly the right age. We had the tow-head blond hair and blue eyes they were looking for.

Some people may call it coincidence or a lucky draw, but I believe God orchestrated the whole scene. The Lord used the blind Sam Shelby to help Charles, and He arranged Baby Grace's fateful lunch date. God is always working out the plan He formed in the beginning, always purposefully unfolding what's meant to be—in your life and in mine.

"Before I shaped you in the womb, I knew all about you.
Before you saw the light of day, I had holy plans for you."

JEREMIAH 1:5 MSG

❧———————— • ————————☙

*Do you believe God carefully plans all the details of our
lives? When have you seen a glimpse of His plan for you?*

3

NASTY NELLIES

"Country girls."

—Nellie Oleson

Nasty Nellies always seem to appear when we are especially insecure and our courage is less than lion-like. Nellie Oleson's words weren't untrue on the Ingallses' first day of school, but the way she said them snatched away Laura's courage. First days of school are uncomfortable enough without a Nasty Nellie running around, stripping people of much-needed confidence.

My first day of high school mirrored Laura's—we both felt uncertain of ourselves. As I walked to school I was terrified. My twin sister and a new girl, who had just moved to town, were beside me. Agreeing where to meet for lunch, we rushed to class as the first bell rang.

Four hours later, we searched for a place to eat far from the cafeteria and my old group of friends. A spiritual change that summer left me unsure of how to act around them. Instead of being brave and sharing my new faith, I was hiding out.

We settled on a grassy patch and ate our lunches. The sun shone bright, and I finally began to relax. As I balled up my empty lunch sack, a girl came running over. She had blond hair and a loud and rude demeanor—so like Nellie.

She looked at us in disgust and sneered, "Freshmen." I'll never forget the look on her face. It wasn't what she said, but the way she said it made our hearts sink. She might as well have been wearing a big bow on top of her head, one that matched her outfit—just like Nellie.

It's been almost twenty-five years since then, and I am finally learning to be bold. I'm not as concerned about what others think. My lifetime of stories about God are pouring out of me. When a Nasty Nellie tries to discourage you, remember Laura. Don't stick out your tongue the way Laura did, but know in your heart that your experiences are more powerful than mean words. You may not think bravery is in your bones, but God will give you the strength to be courageous when you trust Him.

> "This is my command—be strong and courageous! Do not be afraid or discouraged. For the LORD your God is with you wherever you go."
>
> JOSHUA 1:9 NLT

Have you ever encountered a Nasty Nellie? How do hurtful people drain your courage? What can you do to ignite courage in yourself and in someone else?

4
_____

DECLARATIONS OF LOVE

"Nothing bad comes from telling people how you feel."
—CHARLES INGALLS

E xpressing our feelings can be scary. We often hide our emotions to protect ourselves. Laura is crushed when her feelings for a boy are recorded on a talking machine and then played for the entire school. Charles tries to make her feel better and says it's good to share her feelings with others. He says people want to know they are loved, needed, and cared for. It takes courage to tell someone what's happening inside us. The telling is never a wrong choice, even if it doesn't always end the way we hope.

I wanted to say those three little words, wanted to tell Josh how I felt my whole world belonged by his side. But I was scared he'd look back at me with an empty expression and smile awkwardly. When I finally found the courage to speak, I found out he'd been waiting all along for me to say "I love you" before he did. My courage sparked his.

My husband is a quiet guy. He talks a bit more than our goldfish. It's not that he doesn't have anything to say, but he weighs his words. He's careful with what comes out of his mouth. Not me. I throw words around like a pizza chef throws dough. It can be quite a mess sometimes, and then again words spoken from the heart can start something wonderful.

God's declarations of love are all around us. He expresses His love through nature and people, and mostly through His Word. And while not all love stories are dependable, His is. God demonstrated His love through Jesus. He made the first move, proclaiming the words of love by sending His Son to die. All so we could know Him.

Charles advises Laura not to hide her feelings, even if she is embarrassed and doesn't know how the boy will respond. Telling God how we feel is a completely different experience. We don't have to wait for the right timing or the perfect words. We can fling adoration and praise all over the place. He delights in hearing how much we love Him. In the end, the boy, Jason, openly confesses his love to Laura in front of the entire class. It's a bold declaration, but not nearly as bold as God's love for us.

> This is real love—not that we loved God, but that he loved us and sent his Son as a sacrifice to take away our sins. Dear friends, since God loved us that much, we surely ought to love each other.
>
> 1 JOHN 4:10–11 NLT

Are you often afraid to share your feelings? You can ask God to make you brave enough to talk about your feelings when you need to.

5

FLYING HIGH

"For the first time in my life, I feel alive."
—DOC BAKER

L ove has a way of igniting new life in us. It makes us smile so big that our cheeks hurt and the joy inside feels as if it might burst out through our skin. It's as if we're flying among the clouds. Walnut Grove's Dr. Baker had this experience when he met Kate. She was young and full of life. He didn't know what he saw in him. But she loved him, and that gave Dr. Baker a feeling he'd never experienced.

A few years ago, I felt the same way when I opened my eyes after brain surgery. I emerged from that experience with a new story of God's abundant faithfulness and goodness. Energy bubbled out of me that a seven-year-old boy couldn't match. Boisterous, animated words tumbled out of my mouth, dripping with hope. And even as the pain-killers wore off, the joy did not fade.

I knew after surviving this surgery that God had given me a story of His outrageous love—a story I can't help but share. It's too glorious not to. I believe Jesus wants us to live with an excitement for life—the way Doc Baker was changed because of his love for Kate.

Years of loneliness often precede heart-awakening love. Health challenges are sometimes the stepping-stones to unfathomable renewal. If you're in a difficult situation, keep seeking God through His Word. He will strengthen you. And if you are flying in the clouds, thank God every day and tell someone how you got there.

"A thief has only one thing in mind—he wants to steal, slaughter, and destroy. But I have come to give you everything in abundance, more than you expect—life in its fullness until you overflow!"

JOHN 10:10 TPT

Think of a time when you felt a new excitement for life. What sparked the change? How can you take a step toward feeling alive today?

6

NOT A MAGIC CURE

"I'm afraid that's too little, too late, Mrs. Oleson.
The harm's already been done."
—CAROLINE INGALLS

A pologies don't erase what's been said or done. They may help soothe hurt feelings or clarify the real intention, but saying "I'm sorry" isn't a magic cure for relationship or emotional damage. It's not that easy. Harriet Oleson has been slandering the people of Walnut Grove in the town newspaper. Caroline confronts her about the gossip and rumors, but an apology can't repair the destruction she's caused. Hurtful words aren't always malicious, but apologies don't solve the problem every time.

I was engaged my last semester of college. It seemed every friend bought me a bridal magazine. I had already purchased my wedding dress, so I'm not sure why *Modern Bride's Best Dresses of 1999* was on our coffee table. One day, flipping through the pages, I asked my fiancé if he liked a certain dress.

When it comes to fashion or decorating, my husband is super-opinionated. The thing is, he usually doesn't say anything unless I ask for his impression. I don't know what I thought to gain through this silly interaction, but it didn't go well. I understand now that I was setting him up for inevitable failure.

"It's all right. I guess I'm not crazy about spaghetti straps."

I suspect my face went blank because my wedding dress had spaghetti straps. I got real quiet, and he knew something was wrong. I think he would have eaten the entire magazine if it meant he could take the words back. But he couldn't. Spaghetti straps and a million other silly things often lead to hurt feelings.

Restoring a damaged relationship is tricky. Going back is impossible; the future is our only hope. Somehow my fiancé managed to repair the damage. He used the same opinionated spirit to tell me how beautiful I looked on our wedding day. He never even mentioned my gorgeous dress. Smart man.

No amount of apologizing or convincing can change the words we say. Instead, the solution is to change the dialogue. If Mrs. Oleson could stop saying sorry and start being kind, her words could redeem a relationship. Hurt feelings are unavoidable, but communicating with love is the solution.

Most important of all, continue to show deep love for each other, for love covers a multitude of sins.

1 PETER 4:8 NLT

When someone hurts you with words, is an apology
enough to bring forgiveness? Or is it the person's
love that ushers you to a place of grace?

7

HIGH AND LOWS

*"You mustn't be afraid to hurt, because that is part
of life. Hurt is something you measure happiness by.
It's like valleys and mountain peaks. Without them
both, the world would be flat and uninteresting."*
—CAROLINE INGALLS

Life can be unbelievably heartbreaking. Sadness is all around us. The hurts of this world are deep and painful: Mothers who won't meet their babes. Families torn apart by divorce, and cancer taking the lives of those we love. Hurricanes and fires and shootings. Why does it often seem that the valleys plunge deeper than the mountains are high?

I've had my share of tough times. You may have an unimaginable story of pain. While we all experience difficulties, I find myself assuming life is supposed to be smooth and predictable. This couldn't be further from the truth. The world is not one big, flat prairie. It's a tempting thought, but Ma convinces Laura otherwise. Every hurt is a valley resting in the shadows of a great mountain peak.

God's best work has taken place during my most challenging times. When I have nowhere else to turn, God walks beside me and makes me stronger. Maybe our valleys exist to reveal how desperately we need Him. Persevering through trials produces endurance to help us reach the mountain peak. Overwhelmed with gratitude, our hearts soar as we look back at the trail we've blazed.

Now I can find the hidden joy in the reflections of the difficulties of my life—all the hard, beautiful gifts He has allowed me to experience. We can be thankful for the good and the bad, grateful for His presence in the valleys and up on the heights. God repeatedly surprises us with a beautiful landscape of various highs and lows.

As Caroline said, life will never be all-prairie. We wouldn't want it to be. The valleys make the mountain peaks even more breathtaking.

> Consider it all joy, my brethren, when you encounter various trials, knowing that the testing of your faith produces endurance.
>
> JAMES 1:2–3 NASB

How would you describe the landscape of your life?
What are the greatest lessons you have learned
traveling through the valleys? Thank God for
working in the diverse terrains of your life.

8

JOY WILL FOLLOW

*"Guess I got kinda jealous, you
being so smart and all."*
—LAURA INGALLS

If we're not careful, the green-eyed monster of jealousy sometimes slips out of its cave and runs rampant. It longs for more stuff, more recognition, and deeper connections, and it starts when we're young. In this episode, Laura is jealous when Mary is selected to represent Walnut Grove for the state mathematics test. She can't help but wish she had been chosen.

I've wished to be chosen too. My first jealous moment happened while watching a Christmas episode of *Little House on the Prairie*! I was four years old, my eyes glued to the television set at my grandmother's house. I'll never forget waiting to watch myself on the screen, the Little House full of presents to open, those fat striped sticks of peppermint to wrap our lips around, and a snowy window scene with all the kids cheering as Pa snowshoes across the white expanse to the barn. My twin sister and I had one other scene in the script—falling asleep on Ma's lap. Neither of us volunteered to sleep.

On the set, we did as we were told even if it meant disappointment later on. When twins share a role, one is on the set filming while the other waits in the dressing room. We had no idea which part we would get to play. I remember the arguing beforehand, but then the episode was over, we forgot about it, and we moved on.

We were sitting in front of the television when the familiar *Little House* theme song began. And there I sat—through a full hour of jealousy. My sister Brenda unwrapped beautiful gifts and huddled with the family around the open window up in the loft and ran her tongue over striped sugar. I got the sleeping scene.

I'd like to tell you I got over it. But that wouldn't be true. I've struggled with jealousy most of my life. Life is challenging when you want what someone else has.

Jealousy tells only half the story: it emphasizes what we can't grasp. And it ignores everything God has given us. God knows when we feel forgotten. He loves us without the slightest hesitation but desires us to be content. If we can embrace contentment, joy will follow. On the show, Laura finally admits to Mary that jealousy caused her bad behavior, and she apologizes. She decides to be thankful for what she already has.

> Godliness with contentment is great gain. . . . If we have food and clothing, we will be content with that.
>
> 1 TIMOTHY 6:6, 8 NIV

With whom have you experienced jealousy? How can you embrace contentment today?

SEASON 2, EPISODE 2, "FOUR EYES"

9

THE POWER OF WORDS

*"That old saying isn't true, about sticks
and stones. Names do hurt."*

—CHARLES INGALLS

W ords can wound us. Negatively labeling others is more damaging than a stick any day. Nellie Oleson's taunting is more than Mary can bear. She avoids being criticized about her new glasses by hiding them in a log. Pa forgives Mary for lying and encourages her to focus on the good that comes from wearing spectacles.

I can't remember anyone calling me a name when I was growing up. But my group of fifth-grade friends and I thought a little too highly of ourselves. I didn't realize what we were doing to one of our classmates.

The girl's mom called to explain the situation. She said we were making her daughter feel rejected and not good enough to be included in our group. She called my sister and me, the meanest girls in school, *bullies*. I don't remember if we called the girl a name—like "Four Eyes"—but I do know she felt rejected. We were interested in making a name for ourselves and imagined this girl getting in the way. After we apologized, her mom told us never to speak to her daughter again.

I never did, even when I had a class with her in high school. Avoiding all eye contact was my strategy. I blame it on bully guilt.

Our words are powerful. They can build up and tear down. They can demonstrate love one moment and hate the next. I wish we could bridle our tongues to be used only for good. But God didn't design us that way. Instead He gave us the Holy Spirit to live inside us. He convicts us of sin, gives us remorse, and humbles us so we can grow in character.

We all trip on our words sometimes. It seems to happen most when we want to be known; maybe that's why Nellie resorted to name-calling. The Holy Spirit is our only hope for healing. Instead of promoting self, with the Spirit's help we shift our thinking to promote God, living every day to make *His* name known.

> With our tongues we bless our God and Father; with the same tongues we curse the very men and women he made in his image. Curses and blessings out of the same mouth! My friends, this can't go on.
>
> JAMES 3:9–10 MSG

Have you hurt someone with your words? What could you do to restore a relationship damaged by unkind remarks? Do your words make His name known or yours?

10

WHERE HELP IS FOUND

*"With the two of us believing, I'd say
we have a pretty good start."*
—LAURA INGALLS

Any road is easier to navigate with two hearts believing together. When someone stands with us, we can take turns supporting each other. A friend or partner can make all the difference in the world.

When the baseball team of Walnut Grove takes on the neighboring city of Sleepy Eye, Charles Ingalls hopes to win. Their chances are slim to none, based on last year's final score. But Laura and Pa believe in the impossible, and they pray for help. When they see Mr. Mumford throw a rock at a chicken-hawk, their prayers are answered.

Months after marrying my husband, I was lonely and unhappy. He worked long hours as a college soccer coach. I found myself constantly waiting for him to pull in the driveway. He saw the struggle and offered to leave a job he loved so we could move closer to my family. His willingness to sacrifice proved every spoken wedding vow.

The night we drove away, I felt terrible for making him leave. As we parked in front of our new rental, I could see his spirits tank. The pumpkin-orange countertops in the kitchen and the bright blue water heater across from our bed didn't help the situation.

We had to start over, believing God would take care of us. I searched the help-wanted ads immediately, eager to show Josh how

grateful I was for his sacrifice. Securing a job quickly felt impossible, but we knew if we kept believing together, God would show up just in time. A job became available at the perfect moment, a little like Mr. Mumford throwing that rock days before the big game. We celebrated our victory and the reality of two being better than one became a cemented theme in our marriage.

Laura and her pa believed together, and it gave them strength and faith even when the odds were against them. God's comforting help is often found in the person He put right beside you.

It's better to have a partner than go it alone. Share the work, share the wealth.

ECCLESIASTES 4:9 MSG

Think of a time when you had to hold on to someone and believe God for the rest. How is it easier to believe when you have someone beside you?

11

THE PURPOSE OF PAIN

"God gives you pain to make you quit
whatever it is you're doing, kind of a signal.
If a person don't heed it, then he's going
to get himself in a heap of trouble."
—DOC BAKER

A re you the kind of person who pushes through pain? Going to the doctor may seem like a waste of time, but pain has a purpose. In the past, I ignored my symptoms and hoped for the best. Dr. Baker would have been disappointed in me as his patient, likely telling me, as he did Albert, to listen closely to my body or trouble would come calling.

The month before I found out about my brain tumor, I was in a heap of trouble. Terrible headaches kept me up at night, bouts of dizziness left me uneasy, and my zeal for life was gone. I chalked it up to stress and a past neck injury. Self-diagnosis is never a good idea. By the time my doctor ordered the brain scan, I was desperate.

Pain is our body's way of communicating with us. God speaks through physical suffering, telling us to slow down or get help. I've learned my lesson. I take it easy when my head hurts! Dr. Baker reminds Albert to take pain seriously, even when the world demands he keep going. His football coach wanted him to play even though he was hurting, and ignoring his pain resulted in two broken ribs. Usually the quickest road to recovery requires time to rest, but with so much to do we are tempted to ignore our bodies and keep pushing. Listen to pain, trust what your body is telling you, and seek trustworthy help.

> Trust GOD from the bottom of your heart; don't try to figure out everything on your own. Listen for GOD's voice in everything you do. . . . Your body will glow with health, your very bones will vibrate with life!
>
> PROVERBS 3:5–6, 8 MSG

Do you think God speaks through your pain? Is He telling you to slow down or get help?

12
_____

LOVE MAKES
US NEW

"He's not too short; I'm too tall."
—NELLIE OLESON

L ove changes us. Behaviors and attitudes we once clung to are transformed when our hearts beat for someone special. Instead of picking out his or her faults, we begin to see our part in the equation. Nellie Oleson's actions had always reflected a very self-centered person. But Nellie had never been in love. Percival's coming to town not only rescues Nellie's restaurant, it sets her free from a lifetime of bitterness. Love changes her perspective.

Falling in love with Jesus can be a similar experience. As a teenager, I felt the Lord drawing me to Himself. I'd never been in love, but I wanted to change. I wanted to live for someone other than myself. The fullness of God's love overwhelmed my heart and trickled down to my toes. I began to put my opinions aside and humbly walk in relationship with Him.

As I learned to love God more, my selfish actions became apparent. Like Nellie, I was willing to admit my faults because love can change us. God's unconditional love is irresistible. It humbles us and alters our perspectives, and we are made new. The greatest love the world has ever known changes everything.

If anyone is in Christ, he is a new creature; the old things
passed away; behold, new things have come.

2 CORINTHIANS 5:17 NASB

*Have you changed after falling in love with
someone? How do you imagine God changing
your life when you give Him your heart?*

13

QUESTIONING GOD

"Why did God let my wife and daughter die?"
—MR. EDWARDS

Even today, I wouldn't have a quick or simple answer to Mr. Edwards's question. When his family died of scarlet fever, he turned his back on God. Charles wanted Mr. Edwards to join the Ingalls family at church, but he just couldn't get himself to go.

Our questions are important—they help us communicate with God. I no longer fear asking because I know God can handle our questions. He wants us to ask! Questions begin conversations with Him. And that's what He's after—a relationship with us.

Loss has a way of emboldening our spirits, doesn't it? In the Bible, Moses boldly answered God with a question in Exodus 3:11. "Who am I to go to the king and lead your people out of Egypt?" (CEV). And David, while waiting, asked the Lord, "How long will it be?" (Psalm 6:3). Even Jesus asked, "My God, my God, why have you forsaken me?" while hanging on the cross (Matthew 27:46 NIV).

The first time I questioned God was about my Grandma Lou. Cancer had already taken my grandpa, and Grandma and I enjoyed a special connection beyond sharing the name Lou.

Grandma Lou died in a car accident during a spontaneous trip to the mountains with friends. Especially with a major loss, we often question God's goodness. How can a loving God allow such a terrible event? Why would He let us face such sadness?

Losing my grandma forced me to surrender to God's will. I opened my tight grip and started trusting Him to lead the way, even if the road was rough. The lessons I learned prepared me for future challenges.

God is bigger than our questions, bigger than our troubles. He sees every detail and knows that every tragedy has a purpose. We may never understand the reason for our suffering. Our hearts may feel forever broken. But when our souls ache, and we have questions on our lips, we see our need for Jesus. The questioning is what eventually brought Mr. Edwards to his knees and back to God. When we question we can fully engage—with our hearts open—to receive His comfort.

I have told you these things, so that in me you may have peace. In this world you will have trouble. But take heart! I have overcome the world.

JOHN 16:33 NIV

What hard questions have you asked God? How have the tragedies of your life led you closer to Him?

14

LOVE FROM
THE START

"Did you fall in love at first sight?"
—Mary Ingalls

I used to laugh at the idea of "love at first sight." How could love possibly begin in just one glance? My husband disagrees. Josh believes love is a calm sense of assurance that the relationship could be forever if both parties were willing. It was his experience when he first saw me, so how could I argue?

Mary Ingalls wanted to hear all about her parents falling in love. She hoped it was instant attraction.

I can't speak for Michael Landon's personal relationships, but as a director he definitely believed in love at first sight. At the NBC corporate office, Michael took one look at my sister and me and said, "Those are my girls." He loved us instantly.

The crazy thing about God is that He doesn't wait until we're born to start loving us. His love began before the beginning of time. He loves us as no one else could. Caroline tells Mary how she loved Charles from the moment she saw him. It's just the way God loves you and me, but He does it even better.

You saw me before I was born. Every day of my life was recorded in your book. . . . How precious are your thoughts about me, O God. They cannot be numbered!

PSALM 139:16–17 NLT

Do you believe in love at first sight? How does it make you feel to know God loved you even before you were born?

15

TAKE A BREAK

*"The first thing I'm going to do is go
fishing. Alone, where it's quiet."*

—NELS OLESON

After living above the Winoka saloon for months, Nels is eager to return to Walnut Grove for some peace and quiet. We all need time to be alone. Too few of us practice solitude these days. Surrounded by constant interaction and noise, we seldom let our minds rest. Wouldn't we all benefit from a mental break from time to time?

My husband has a jam-packed schedule—most of us do. His commute is the only alone time he has every day. While I'd been taking time away since the kids were born, he never had. I knew he would benefit from some solo time, where he could think without interruptions or responsibilities.

After much convincing, he headed out on his first Man Weekend. He spent a few days in a cabin near Yosemite, all by himself. He could do whatever he wanted, sleep until he woke up, and enjoy the silence. From there, he traveled up north to visit a friend from grade school. This guy makes my husband laugh more than anyone else on the planet. And while laughter is not quiet, in a way it can be just as nourishing and often leads to deep conversations when we have time to connect.

I can't tell you how refreshed his face looked as we huddled around him for a welcome-home hug. His eyes glistened with life and energy. He let out a deep breath.

"That was wonderful. I need to do it every year."

We all need a getaway. Solitude gives us the chance to be quiet so God can fill us back up. It's difficult to hear God speak over the noise of everyday life, especially in our crazy house. Even Jesus had to get away to hear from His Father.

Whether it's hiking through the mountains, walking on the beach, or fishing like Nels, find a place to be alone. A place away from the distractions of life. When we are alone with the Lord, we are able to collect His blessings of peace.

> After He had sent the crowds away, He went up on the mountain by Himself to pray; and when it was evening, He was there alone.
>
> MATTHEW 14:23 NASB

Where do you go to be alone? Do you give yourself and those you love permission to enjoy a retreat?

16
_____

BIRTHDAY WISHES

"I don't have anything to wish for. I have everything
in the world, right here in this room."
—MARY INGALLS

As we grow older, our birthday lists tend to grow shorter. The things—possessions—we once wanted so badly are no longer as important as they used to be. We value experiences and quality time with people more than beautifully wrapped packages. On her sixteenth birthday, Mary Ingalls could have wished for any number of things, but she didn't. The table surrounded by loved ones left her eyes full of tears, and she was speechless and soul-content.

I remember that same feeling during my eighteenth birthday party. Instead of traditional gifts, the guests were secretly instructed to bring eighteen things of their choosing for my twin sister and me. Overwhelmed by the huge pile of presents, we envisioned making a pretty good haul.

We did, but not in the way we thought. I'll never forget opening eighteen Q-tips and eighteen quarters for the laundry machines at college. We opened gifts of eighteen hair ties and pencils and stamped envelopes so we could write home. Of all the crazy things we opened, my favorite came from a friend from our junior high days. She'd found eighteen notes we had written to her on ruled binder paper. They were folded in crazy shapes that only junior high girls would make.

Poring over the notes, I laughed and cried. Some my sister and I read out loud, and others we tucked away for later. They brought unforgettable experiences back to life for a few hours that day. As I looked around at all the faces at the party—people who cared about my sister and me and had built relationships with us—I knew I had received the single best gift.

Love.

The simplest gifts are usually the most valuable to us. Like Mary, we cherish people and places and time spent together. Tears of joy on monumental birthdays mean more to us than any gift ever could.

Then our mouth was filled with laughter, and our tongue with joyful shouting; then they said among the nations, "The LORD has done great things for them." The LORD has done great things for us; we are glad.

PSALM 126:2–3 NASB

What is the best birthday gift you ever received?
When you think back on a birthday, do you remember
the gifts or the people you saw that day?

17

HOLD STILL AND LISTEN

"If you'd hold still for a minute, I'd tell you."
—LAURA INGALLS

O ur lives and schedules are full. We zip from one task to the next, hoping to accomplish everything on our to-do list while longing to discover purpose in it all. I've found myself, when speeding around, asking God to reveal His will for my life. Will God instruct us while we're multitasking? Laura had an idea for how they could surprise Mary, but Albert wouldn't stop talking and cleaning the stalls to hear her out. Laura encouraged Albert to hold still, in much the same way that God asks us to "be still, and know" (Psalm 46:10 KJV).

Sometimes life forces us to stop. That happened to me when I was diagnosed with a brain tumor. Immediately, every plan, every item on my to-do list that didn't have to do with healing was put on hold. Suddenly I had time to think and pray. It proved to be a season during which God whispered all kinds of promises to me through His Word and through His people. But mostly, I heard Him in the stillness.

One of our greatest challenges when we're before the Lord is learning to be quiet—to stop talking. Stop asking. There are times when pouring out our hearts is necessary. At other times, silence gives way to the simplest, most authentic connection. We will never know what the Lord has to tell us if we don't cease our constant chatter. How much direction might I have missed before my surgery experience because I didn't stop to listen?

Since recovering from my brain surgery, I'm in motion most of the time. Now I'm constantly striving to find more quiet. Our homes aren't always the best places for silence, especially if kids are around.

When I need peace, I go to the beach. There's something about taking in the beauty of creation that inspires stillness in me. To sit and watch the waves, waiting for the colors to erupt as the sun dips down: for me it is the perfect place to listen.

It's not easy for us to put our agendas aside and be quiet. It takes sacrifice and discipline on our part. Yet God has so much to tell us in the silence. Just as Laura said, hold still and let Him tell you.

> The Lord GOD, the Holy One of Israel, has said, "In repentance and rest you will be saved, in quietness and trust is your strength."
>
> ISAIAH 30:15 NASB

Do you have a hard time being still before the Lord?
Where is the best place for you to be quiet? Challenge
yourself to spend even a few minutes in silence today.

1 8

BELIEVING A LIE

*"I know that what I'm afraid of is not
out there—it's inside me."*
—Adam Kendall

F ear is a liar. It creates unthinkable scenes in our heads and tricks us into thinking they are true. They aren't real threats, but we struggle to differentiate between fear and reality. Adam, a blind man, recognizes the difference. He knows fear isn't in the storms of life that he can't see; it comes from within. My problem usually isn't what's happening; it's believing a lie.

Shortly after getting married, I found myself struggling with irrational fears. I never wanted to be alone, especially at night. If my husband knew he'd be late, I'd have to make plans or resort to being scared. There wasn't any reason to be frightened. We lived in a safe neighborhood, and the locks on our doors and windows worked just fine. Maybe it's that my mind wasn't a safe place.

Our minds have a way of recounting every story or scary movie depicting our fears. Satan works like that—grabbing hold of our thoughts, making things we have heard or seen seem real. And then we are paralyzed with fear, as if a frightening person really is at the back door. The only culprit is fear, hijacking our minds.

I didn't know it at the time, but my twin sister also dealt with fear. We talked about it on a weekend sisters' trip. She convinced me that living with fear might be worse than actually facing danger.

Standing up to your thoughts and challenging their validity takes the power away from the evil one.

The first thing I do is command, out loud in a strong voice, the creator of all lies to leave my mind. I pray for the helmet of salvation to guard my thoughts. If I'm a child of God, what can man do to me? Then I ask for the courage to face my fears. With a hefty Maglite in hand, I find out if there's reason to panic. In addition to illuminating the darkness, the Mag could double as a great club, if needed.

When we realize that fear comes from within, we can be confident the way Adam was. Our minds are stronger when we trust Jesus to protect us. Give Him the power over your thoughts. Living without fear frees us, like Adam, to fully live.

> Embrace the power of salvation's full deliverance, like a helmet to protect your thoughts from lies. And take the mighty razor-sharp Spirit-sword of the spoken Word of God.
>
> EPHESIANS 6:17 TPT

Does fear battle with reality in your mind? How do you overcome fear? Do you use the helmet of salvation to guard your thoughts?

19

WHEN HEAVEN COMES TOO SOON

"It's good up in heaven. Jesus is there."

—CARRIE INGALLS

We probably don't think of heaven as often as we should or think of it the way God does. We want the people we love to end up in heaven—just not yet. When Charles Ingalls's mother passes away, his father can't see past this earth. Carrie, with her four-year-old faith, points out how great heaven is. The simple wisdom of a child can reframe our grief.

My stepdad died of a heart attack in 2006. He was only fifty-eight. I happened to be with him, but I couldn't save him. As the paramedics loaded the stretcher into the ambulance, I cried on the phone with my sister. She drove straight over, and then we headed to the hospital, praying for a miracle.

My nephew was in the back, strapped into his car seat. We talked freely, not shielding anything from his little four-year-old ears. I don't think I fully realized he was back there, listening. As we pulled into the parking lot, trying our best to gather ourselves into something presentable, he spoke up.

"If Grandpa Lanny is going to heaven, why are you both so sad?"

He said it plainly, almost confused by our actions. Through blurry eyes and with tear-stained cheeks, we turned to face our little prophet. Apparently he had been paying attention during Sunday school. He knew that if someone believed in Jesus, he or she would go to heaven after death. We believed, but our sadness seemed to leak out of every pore.

We were sad to lose our dad and a grandpa for our kids. We were worried for my mom, who was now a widow. Our hearts were breaking as we thought of Christmas and Father's Day and lake trips without him. Sometimes heaven seems to come too soon.

Saying good-bye to someone you love is never easy, especially when it is unexpected. Our only comfort is heaven. Gaining the perspective of a child, like Carrie or my nephew, gives us peace to grieve and keep living.

To me, living means living for Christ, and dying is even better.

PHILIPPIANS 1:21 NLT

Have you ever had a child share spiritual wisdom with you?
How does the hope of heaven comfort you in your sadness?

20

IT BEGINS WITH A DREAM

"You are riding the wind; I'm just riding a hay wagon."
—MR. EDWARDS

God orchestrates various seasons in our lives; some are dream-chasing seasons and others are not. When John Jr. receives a college scholarship to pursue a career in writing, Mr. Edwards senses his son will never be a farmer like him. Dreams change as we age. God creates new opportunities that send us in fresh directions, but often we must wait as His divine plan reveals itself.

My dream job of becoming a mom proved to be harder than I ever imagined. Wiping runny noses and enduring tantrums at the park was exhausting. My personality was swallowed up by piles of laundry to fold. Matching socks and picking up Cheerios day after day wasn't the hang-up—I'd wanted to stay home with my children. I just never expected it to be so all-consuming. I was lonely and so tired. Dreaming was out of the question. Survival took up too much time and energy.

Scrolling through social media, I'd see other women making their mark on the world. I wanted to make a mark, but my ink was dry. Then I realized that comparing ourselves to others silences the extraordinary stories we are living. When I'm not dreaming, I start comparing. Like Mr. Edwards, my life felt similar to working a hay wagon. I needed a new gust of wind to ride upon. A new dream to work toward.

The calling God has planned for each of us is waiting to be revealed. His timing unfolds exactly as it should. If I could have seen what was in store, the reward patience had to offer, I would have been at peace even in the middle of the piles of laundry. Every day at home was a dream come true, but it also ushered me toward finding a new dream.

Every worthwhile dream begins with a dreamer. Are you dreaming right now? Maybe your dream is like that of John Jr.—pursuing a career, going to college, and becoming a writer. Maybe it's learning to knit or starting a business or redecorating your home. Whatever it is, life sometimes delays our dreams. But don't give up! God wants us to dream.

When we wait for His perfect timing, He rewards our hearts with joy as the dream comes true. Then our joy is doubled as we share the story of His favor and the road we walked to accomplish our dreams.

When the LORD restored the fortunes of Zion, we were like those who dream.

PSALM 126:1 NIV

Do you have a dream in your heart? How can you see God working through your daily routine to prepare you for it?

2 1

THE REMEDY

"We just have to pray, with all our hearts."
—Laura Ingalls

Worry can consume us, especially when someone we love is seriously ill. At times there isn't much we can do *but* pray. I haven't always felt that my prayers were enough. I've wanted to do more. But heartfelt prayers are the best possible gift we can give.

While Charles and the children are away on a trip, a dangerous infection begins to form on Caroline's leg. Cutting the trip short, they find Caroline collapsed in the house and quickly fetch Dr. Baker. The uncertainty of her condition gives the whole family quite a scare. Laura bows her head in urgent pleading for her ma to recover.

I've been on the receiving side of prayers. There is nothing as powerful or comforting to give someone walking a hard road. Thousands of people were praying for me during my brain surgery, praying that I would survive, that I would remember the past and my loving family.

The raging battle in my mind tormented me most, teetering back and forth between anxiety and trust. The one thing I needed was peace. I asked everyone I knew to pray for it. I can't begin to explain it, but I rode on the wings of prayer. I have never experienced such calm in a very intense situation.

I learned that prayer is not our last resort, it is our first and most important resource. Laura's praying was the best thing she could have done. When we're worried about something or someone, prayer is the remedy. We do our best to pray not for things and quick fixes, but for character and wisdom and the strength to persevere through difficult times. It helps us surrender to God's will and keeps our minds focused on eternity.

Don't worry about anything; instead, pray about everything. Tell God what you need, and thank him for all he has done. Then you will experience God's peace, which exceeds anything we can understand. His peace will guard your hearts and minds as you live in Christ Jesus.

PHILIPPIANS 4:6–7 NLT

⊹ ———————— • ———————— ⊹

What do you pray for? Do you realize that your prayers are powerful? How does prayer lead to surrender in your life?

2 2

JUST BE YOU

"You just be you, Laura Ingalls.
Apparently that's what he
liked in the first place."
—Caroline Ingalls

Oftentimes we may try to be someone we aren't, which is like wearing a friend's shoes that are two sizes too small . . . or too big. In this episode, Caroline reminds her daughter to be herself; it's the only sensible way to live.

During our first few days on the set of *Little House*, my mom tried to keep my sister and me from crying on camera. Michael Landon pulled her aside to ease her mind. "I don't know who Baby Grace is, and you don't know who Baby Grace is. Let's let Wendi and Brenda figure it out." Michael wanted Baby Grace to be herself. It's the only practical way to create a character for television, and less stressful too.

In real life, being anything different from who God created you to be is extremely hard work. All that effort is wasted because ultimately, we can never authentically be anything but ourselves.

The Creator of the world knew what He was doing when He made you and me. He wants each of us to be the person He designed. We forget that Father God is a master artist, He doesn't make mistakes. Laura needed to hear it, and so do we.

GOD, you are our Father. We're the clay and you're our potter: All of us are what you made us.

ISAIAH 64:8 MSG

Have you ever tried to be someone other than who you are? How much effort did it take? What did God create you to do that no one else can?

23

A MIND-SET

"I'm a farmer and I love it, and I'm a father
and I love it. And best of all, I'm married
to Caroline Ingalls and I love her."
—Charles Ingalls

Contentment is being thankful for our lives and what we have. It's easier said than done; contentment doesn't come naturally. When Charles and Caroline attend a class reunion, they see their old friends are successful but discontent. Reflecting on his simple life, Charles is struck by how satisfied he is. Contentment does not depend on circumstances, but on our mind-set.

Charles Ingalls reminds me of my stepdad. He was a simple man who worked hard and loved his four girls as well as his wife. A mailman for more than thirty years, my dad sorted letters like seeds, drove his mail truck as if it were a plow, and delivered packages as big as sacks of grain. While rain didn't wipe out his annual salary, it made quite the soggy mess. Being content with a blue-collar job took more than just a good attitude. I think my stepdad's faith played a role. I saw him every dark morning at the kitchen table reading his Bible. He had a deep love for God.

The secret to contentment is to be grounded in Christ. When our hearts and minds are focused on Him, we can't help but be grateful for the lives we've been given. Charles didn't look at his life and see what was lacking. He saw everything as a beautiful gift from

God. Gratitude recognizes how much we have compared to what we deserve. We deserve nothing but have been given everything we need to pursue a life of contentment.

> Godliness with contentment is great gain. For we brought nothing into the world, and we can take nothing out of it.
>
> 1 Timothy 6:6–7 niv

Think of someone you know who demonstrates contentment. What makes him or her content? When your focus is Christ, what changes?

24

OUT OF THE LOFT

*"The thing to do is to get busy for others. The
more you do, the less time you have to hurt."*

—Caroline Ingalls

Hurt often causes us to withdraw. When we're focused on our sadness, we battle self-pity. Serving others can be the best solution. It shifts our attention and allows us to be a blessing to those around us. After Laura's beau, Almanzo, leaves Walnut Grove, Laura takes Ma's advice and travels to Sleepy Eye to help at the school for the blind. It doesn't heal her broken heart, but it does get her out of bed where she can focus her thinking on service rather than suffering.

A hurting or lonely heart can be difficult to overcome. One summer I felt a bit like Laura. My heart hadn't been broken; it just wanted to be loved. My twin sister and my best friend both had boyfriends, and I didn't. My days slowly passed by, like traveling solo across an empty prairie. While I was always welcomed to join my sister and friend, being a third wheel wasn't too appealing.

Camp was a last-minute decision, something my mom suggested. I didn't have anything better to do except feel sorry for myself, so I volunteered to counsel second-graders for a week. Suddenly I had nine little sisters to take care of. They all wanted to sit next to me during meals and chapel. We hiked and made crafts and swam until we were wiped out. And then I answered questions and told stories. I said prayers and comforted the girls who couldn't sleep.

When we get busy helping others, our troubles shrink. The sting of hurt subsides as we shine the spotlight on someone else. Laura's serving at the school was just what she needed. Her washing and cleaning was equivalent to my counseling little girls at camp. And when I returned home, my loneliness didn't feel so overwhelming.

Serving others unites our hearts to people, takes our minds off our troubles, and sometimes starts a process of healing that could only happen through service.

Those who live to bless others will have blessings heaped upon them, and the one who pours out his life to pour out blessings will be saturated with favor.

PROVERBS 11:25 TPT

Do you withdraw in lonely times? How can you take your mind off your problems and serve someone else?

25

COMMUNITY, NOT PERFECTION

"It won't be fancy, but we've got plenty."
—Caroline Ingalls

Perfectionism prevents many of us from opening our homes. The pressure to provide good food in an enjoyable setting overwhelms us. Caroline Ingalls has something to teach us about hospitality. Having people to our homes—large or small, fancy or casual—is about togetherness. Nothing else.

When our kids were young, we didn't get out much. We missed movie dates and quiet nights together, but even more, we missed having people over. Overwhelmed by diapers and laundry, with toys every-where, I didn't have the energy to clean the house and cook a killer dinner for company.

One night Josh said, "Let's start Sunday night dinners at our house."

After my panic subsided, I realized he was speaking wis-dom. He knew we needed encouragement and fun with other couples. So we opened our front door to guests on Sunday eve-nings. We didn't think of these meals as dinner parties, but rather as time to enjoy friends and food. We invited couples and singles to come and hang out. The important thing was not what filled our stomachs, or how spotless the house was, but what filled our hearts.

Some nights a busy schedule or a slim pantry made the idea seem impossible, but it always worked out. I had to resist the urge to over-clean. We didn't need a flawless house. What we needed was people around us, people with a sparkle in their eyes. We longed for conversation around the table, even if we had to step over toys to get there.

I'll never forget those nights: card games and homemade ice cream and lifting up prayers around our big wooden table. Something happens when we do life with other people, when we walk alongside them through life's ups and downs. Our hearts began to beat for those around us, not just ourselves. We prayed fervently for each other and came to the rescue when someone needed help. It was community at its finest.

We are missing out on wonderful fellowship when we let perfectionism keep us from having people over. Caroline's style of hospitality is a good one: simple food with friends is more important than a fancy meal we're too tired to enjoy. Our friends don't see the dusty shelves and baseboards. They long for community, not perfection.

Every believer was faithfully devoted to following the teachings of the apostles. Their hearts were mutually linked to one another, sharing communion and coming together regularly for prayer.

ACTS 2:42 TPT

Do you let perfectionism keep you from inviting people over? Who are the people you would like to fellowship with? Mark your calendar and have some folks over for dinner.

26

SPEAK UP

"Albert doesn't study that much; it just comes easy to him."
—ANDY GARVEY

I grew up thinking I wasn't smart. I did well in school, but learning didn't come easily. My twin sister, on the other hand, was a naturally gifted student. I never felt good enough or smart enough, at least compared to her.

Andy felt the same way about his best friend, Albert. No amount of studying could make his grades soar like his friend's. When we find ourselves in this situation, we often need someone to believe in us—someone to speak up and be proud of us, even if our efforts don't rise to the highest mark.

I found that person in fifth grade—my teacher. He wove lessons of compassion and grace seamlessly with history and English. One day, in the staff lounge, a fellow teacher asked him if he had the "smart twin." Without hesitation and possibly with a smirk of indignation, he answered, "Yes. I have Wendi."

He shared that story with my mom, but she didn't tell me about it until years later. I was struggling through high school, trying to compete with my sister who always came out on top. When my teacher passed away suddenly from cancer, my mom shared the story with me as we were driving to his memorial service. I never got to thank him for standing up for me, but his words helped me through the next two years before graduation.

At times, we all need someone to defend us, someone who believes we are significant, no matter what our accomplishments. Ironically, Albert was the one to stand up for Andy. He defended Andy and exposed the cheater in Nellie Oleson. Let's all speak courage into someone who has to work extra hard—not just in school, but in life. Be on the lookout for people who never feel that they will be good enough or smart enough; they need us.

"Learn to do good. Work for justice. Help the down-and-out. Stand up for the homeless. Go to bat for the defenseless."

ISAIAH 1:17 MSG

Who has stood up for you? How can you help someone who feels "not good enough"?

27

LONG YET RELIABLE

*"If you know your way is best, then
why take a shortcut?"*
—Caroline Ingalls

Shortcuts often don't cut it when we are working toward success. Taking the quickest route can get us into trouble. Charles Ingalls didn't listen to his wife's warning. He forged a short but rugged path to Sleepy Eye, resulting in a lengthy trip. His shortcut cost him time and created embarrassment and frustration.

I can relate to Pa. Shortcuts are so tempting. My biggest shortcut blunder happened when we were spending our anniversary with another couple, exploring the island of Kauai. Our hike began at the famous Ke'e Beach and finished at the Na Pali Coast. To arrive at the stunning shores of Hanakpiai, we stuck to the well-maintained trail.

After taking loads of pictures, we headed back following the same route. Every so often, a side path came into view. We assumed these paths led to a quicker route because of the countless hikers veering from the main trail. I had the grand idea of taking a shortcut. Our friends wanted to stay on the trail, but I persuaded my husband to join me. We decided to make a race out of it; the first couple back would have bragging rights.

All I can say is that we did not win, and our legs were covered with gashes from the sharp jungle plants we were forced to climb through. Consider another misguided shortcut: Abraham and Sarah grew tired of waiting for God's promise of a son, so they came up with a timesaver. The shortcut, having an heir through their servant Hagar (Genesis 16), brought pain and resentment, not only for their family but for generations.

Taking a shortcut to a longed-for result often isn't a good idea. To taste success, we need to stay on the longer yet reliable road. Take Caroline's advice: if you're headed in the right direction, you don't need to take a shortcut.

> "Don't look for shortcuts to God. The market is flooded with surefire, easygoing formulas for a successful life that can be practiced in your spare time. Don't fall for that stuff, even though crowds of people do."
>
> MATTHEW 7:13 MSG

When did you take a quicker route that didn't work out so well? Have you tried to take a shortcut in your relationship with God? What happened?

2 8

STRINGING BEADS

*"We start learning when we are born, and if we are
wise, we won't stop until the good Lord takes us home."*

—Caroline Ingalls

Learning is a lifelong process. It keeps our minds engaged with the world around us. When Laura doesn't want to go to school, Caroline explains that learning is the best choice. Our lives are a continual lesson, and growing in knowledge and character is rewarding.

During our first season on the set, my sister and I spent many hours in our dressing room. Filming required quiet sets, and we weren't always compliant. The older children were either on camera or with Mrs. Fife, the government-appointed teacher.

Sometimes Melissa Gilbert would sneak over to our trailer. We had more scenes with Half-Pint than with any of the other children, and we felt comfortable with her. Melissa even claims to have taught us our first word. We were stringing beads on the floor when one of us said "Bead"—our first shot at learning.

Even now there's so much I don't know about myself and especially about God. To keep learning, I have to be open to instruction and willing to practice. Growing in my knowledge of God has been a steady pursuit.

When we are young, learning is instinctive, but the more we age, the more intentional we have to be. I, for one, intend to take Caroline's advice and never stop learning.

Teach me your way, O LORD, that I may walk in your truth;
give me an undivided heart to revere your name.

PSALM 86:11 NRSV

What is the first thing you remember learning?
What is God teaching you right now?

29

RUNNING YOUR RACE

*"I just wanna run through the trees and not think
about anything but the wind on my face."*
—ADAM KENDALL

I love to run. There's something about my shoes on a gravel path and the breeze against my cheeks that makes me feel unstoppable. It doesn't matter how fast I am or where I'm headed, my goal is to reach the finish. It gives me a feeling of accomplishment and freedom.

When Adam Kendall regained his sight, he wanted to run. His whole world had been dark and now he could see the obstacles and delights in front of him. When Adam ran through the trees, he felt free from his blindness, free to be himself for the first time in years.

Two days after brain surgery, I was supposed to run a half marathon. My training had been cut short by the surgery and I sadly accepted that I could not run the race. That Sunday morning, I woke up from my first full night of sleep in weeks, mentally invigorated—thinking about the marathon. My sister, Brenda, was asleep on the foldout bed in the corner of my recovery room. I hobbled over and shook her awake. "It's race day. I feel like I could run my half marathon." I was confusing physical stamina with mental stamina, an easy mix-up after brain surgery.

In that moment, I decided to tackle a different sort of race. I clutched the metal railing of the bed, pulled myself up, and prepared to take the six steps to the bathroom sink. In my condition, just getting across the room would give me a sense of accomplishment. It wasn't much, but God took every step with me. I decided it was distance enough to earn my finisher's medallion. The course I was on turned out to be a slow walk toward healing.

When I returned home from surgery, a medal from my race was waiting for me. My uncle had crossed the finish line for both himself and me. He felt I deserved an award even though I didn't run. Holding the prize, I felt the excitement of finishing the race myself. My uncle had taken every step for me, as if we were running side by side.

Jesus does the same, keeping pace beside us no matter what race we are running. Adam Kendall ran through the trees while I barely made the walk across the room. The greatest race of our lives, of course, is to eternity. When we get to heaven, our reward will be far greater than any medal around our necks.

> I press on to reach the end of the race and receive the heavenly prize for which God, through Christ Jesus, is calling us.
> PHILIPPIANS 3:14 NLT

*What race are you running? How does
Jesus keep pace with you?*

30

FEAR OR FAITH

"Miss Beadle, where are the children?"
—CAROLINE INGALLS

T hose who care for children shoulder a great responsibility. And when things go wrong, as they often do, fear can rush in. I know it happens to every parent at some point.

Teachers are like parents, except they have more children to keep track of. Miss Beadle felt the weight of responsibility when she unknowingly dismissed the students of Walnut Grove to walk home when a blizzard was coming. When faced with the unknown, we have a choice to make. God tells us to turn our backs on fear and reach for faith.

When my daughter was a toddler, six moms joined us at the beach. The umbrella-lined shore was piled thick with countless towels and coolers. Our kids built sandcastles and jumped over the small waves. We chatted among the dirty hands gripping plastic shovels.

Hours passed, and as we started to pack up, I looked for my children. I saw my son building a castle with a moat, but my daughter was nowhere in sight. All the moms jumped into action. One searched the parking lot, another the playground.

The rest of us joined hands—fear on each face—and walked slowly through the water. My heart rate soared, and I could barely keep the tears back. I expected to find my sweet girl face-down in the water.

I'd like to say God was my strength and that my faith trumped my fear. But I was consumed with panic. I prayed for peace. But seconds later, I wasn't trusting that He knew best. I was upset He might allow an early end to my daughter's life.

True faith silences fear. In every difficult situation, our options lie before us—fear or faith.

I did find my daughter—squatting with five new little friends down the beach, happy as a sand crab, digging. Not all stories have such happy endings. Fear is a natural reaction. But even in the midst of panic, we must hold onto the promise that God is with us and will give us peace.

Choose faith—even when everything is crashing down, even when all hope seems lost. Whether our eyes are on an entire classroom of responsibilities or on just two little munchkins, we can trust the Lord. Faith will always lead to peace.

"I leave the gift of peace with you—my peace. Not the kind of fragile peace given by the world, but my perfect peace. Don't yield to fear or be troubled in your hearts—instead, be courageous!"

JOHN 14:27 TPT

When you are afraid do you choose fear or faith? Can you think of a time when you chose faith even in the midst of great fear?

SERVE GOD, SERVE OTHERS

"Somebody once said there's no reason to be
ashamed of any job, as long as you do your best."
—CAROLINE INGALLS

Have you ever had a job you didn't like? Most of us would answer yes. Maybe the problem was a high-stress work environment or impatient coworkers we didn't enjoy. The schedule may have been grueling or the work uninteresting. In our culture, our first jobs often involve some kind of service. We can feel inferior when serving our peers.

When Caroline accepts a job in Nellie's restaurant, Charles puts his foot down. He doesn't want his wife cooking for their friends and neighbors, then waiting around

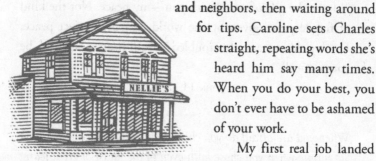

for tips. Caroline sets Charles straight, repeating words she's heard him say many times. When you do your best, you don't ever have to be ashamed of your work.

My first real job landed me in a hot pink shirt with a bright yellow chick on the chest. I welcomed the paycheck, but at sixteen years old, I was embarrassed when friends visited the local fast-food joint. The uniforms only exacerbated how ridiculous I felt, how ashamed that I'd taken a job with such a cheesy uniform. I'd stooped that low. Surrounded by rotisserie ovens and countless poultry hanging by their feet, I was sticky with grease by the end of my nightly shift. In my mind, the lingering scent of chicken on my hands was worse than striped roadkill.

Working hard at menial jobs can be a humbling experience. It puts us in a lower position than we'd like. But at our jobs, humility gives us an accurate view of ourselves. I've found that *lower* is a beautiful place to be. Caroline did it, and Jesus humbled Himself when He came to serve the human race. When we labor with our best effort, we humbly serve God by serving people.

> In your relationships with one another, have the same mindset as Christ Jesus. . . . He made himself nothing by taking the very nature of a servant, being made in human likeness.
>
> PHILIPPIANS 2:5, 7 NIV

What job has humbled you the most? How can you serve God by serving people in your job or in your home?

32

POLISHING SLIDES

"I never thought having babies would be this much fun."
—NELLIE OLESON DALTON

I've always been a playful person, looking for fun around every corner. About the time my son was born, something changed. Pressure to provide and responsibility to parent well left me serious, almost businesslike. I wanted the boat I was sailing to be organized and the young crew prepared to mop the decks. Fun became an afterthought. If all the work was finished, then maybe we could play.

As Nellie said, having babies is a lot of fun. They bring us joy with their cute smiles and silly antics. Many friends and family members played with bubbles and Play-Doh all day with my children, but not me. I was too focused on the parenting part. I learned the hard way that for me, having fun with my kids has to be intentional.

My Grandpa Gordy was the king of fun. He played for endless hours with my sisters and me in the pool and challenged us to games of handball against his garage. He loved taking us to the park. By polishing the slides with Pledge furniture wax, making them extra slippery and fast, he made friends with every child on the playground. At our house, Grandpa would hide money in our dresser drawers. Grandpa Gordy knew how to have fun with kids. I've always wanted to be more like him.

How can we ease the tension between creating stability in our homes and enjoying the children God so graciously gives us? The balancing act is a tricky one. Teaching our children manners and household tasks is valuable, but chores and bedtime are not the details of life that bring us joy.

When I think back to the set of *Little House*, a silly memory often comes to mind. After the long drive through Los Angeles traffic, we would walk through the doors of MGM studios to a beautiful sight. A long table of pink donut boxes welcomed us to work. We started our day with a treat. It's something my grandpa would have done.

I realize moms will never be like grandpas, much less television filming sets, but I do want to have fun with my children. With a playful perspective, life is a candy store of enjoyable experiences to choose from. It doesn't mean we won't work hard, but like Nellie we need to enjoy our kids and head to the park, taking along a can of Pledge.

I recommend having fun, because there is nothing better for people in this world than to eat, drink, and enjoy life. That way they will experience some happiness along with all the hard work God gives them under the sun.

ECCLESIASTES 8:15 NLT

What kind of personality do you have? Do you work first or play? How can you enjoy time with the little people in your life?

33

FALLING PREY TO FALSE GUILT

"You're blaming yourself for what happened,
just like me blaming God for what
happened, and we're both wrong."
—Jonathan Garvey

Pointing fingers is a natural reaction to tragedy. Whose fault was this? When someone dies unexpectedly, survivors look for someone to blame. Many of us accuse God. But perhaps the most difficult blame to resolve is the indictment we place on ourselves. When Alice Garvey and Baby Kendall die in a fire, Albert blames himself. After an intense confession to Mary, Albert runs away. He can't cope with the guilt or forgive himself for the mistake he made.

When my stepdad died of a heart attack, I blamed myself. I was with him that day and called 911 for advice. The operator wanted to send an ambulance, but my stepdad waved it off. His heart stopped beating less than an hour later. For years I held myself responsible for his death. I could have made a different decision that resulted in a very different outcome.

The time I spent blaming myself stripped me of the joy and freedom I had in Christ. Albert and I walked around condemned by no one but ourselves. How do we free ourselves from the guilt of a false step? Running only makes the burden heavier to carry, and hiding is a lonely game. Our heavenly Father never intended us to bear the weight of guilt alone. That's why Jesus came—to save us from our faults, yes, but also from the shame we experience because of them.

Blaming ourselves for someone's death is taking the authority from God. When we wrongly assume the blame, we are falling prey to false guilt. God alone is the Creator of life. Holding our existence is His business, not Albert's or mine. Our hands could never be big enough to do the job justice. He frees us of the blame we are hauling around, fulfilling His purpose along the way.

> Because of the sacrifice of the Messiah, his blood poured out on the altar of the Cross, we're a free people—free of penalties and punishments chalked up by all our misdeeds. And not just barely free, either. Abundantly free!
>
> EPHESIANS 1:7–8 MSG

Have you ever blamed yourself for something only God can control? How does running away only multiply your guilt? Confess and surrender the blame you are shouldering to Jesus.

34

THE BIG RED BARN

"A family all together is the
most special of all."
—LAURA INGALLS

Families celebrate all kinds of events and accomplishments with food as the centerpiece. Those are times when we come together, perhaps from different places or responsibilities, to enjoy one another. When Charles works long hours to surprise Caroline with new dishes, Laura is relieved the family members are all together again. Eating dinner on Pa's hard-earned plates is a real celebration.

Much like the Ingalls family, the cast and crew of *Little House* had a genuine love for one another. We were very much a family and still are. My best memories are of times I was on location at Big Sky Ranch in Simi Valley. I loved visiting the barn animals and playing on the tree swing, but the highlight was lunchtime. Everyone eating together in the big red barn was a family reunion.

Checkered tablecloths covered one side, and the buffet tables ran the full length of the other, with more food choices than a four-year-old could imagine. Visiting with one another as we ate made a lasting impression. It didn't matter what role each person played, from Michael Landon to the extras and the crew.

When we gather around a table, something extraordinary happens. Even a group of friends or coworkers can somehow become as close as kin. Laura was right: families all together are special.

Go and feast on all the good things he has given you.
Celebrate with your family.

DEUTERONOMY 26:11 TLB

*What do you enjoy most about getting together with your
family? Who are the friends who have become family to you?*

35

WISHING FOR WISDOM

"Time spent being angry with you is such a waste."
—CAROLINE INGALLS

L ife can be full of relational conflicts. Our expectations are often unmet, and we let our disappointments turn to anger. This was true for Charles and Caroline Ingalls, just as it's true for us. When Pa misses church one Sunday to rest and work in the fields, Ma is not happy. And she lets him know it.

The days I regret the most are those when I lose my temper. So often it's with my husband or my kids. Why is it that the ones we love the most have to endure the worst of us? Most of the time my anger doesn't do anyone any good. It's just a way to voice my disapproval of not getting what I wanted.

When it's all said and done, the circumstances that upset us don't really matter. The backstory will soon be forgotten. Even justified anger can be a meaningless waste of time if we allow our tempers to boil. What matters is the condition of our hearts and the tone we set for our lives and for our families.

Allowing ourselves to be governed by our anger can be a damaging cycle, and it can be hard to escape. Losing our tempers offers no great reward. We're left with guilt and shame over what we've said, over what we've done. We have this sick, selfish feeling inside. We're disappointed in ourselves, wishing we had the wisdom to catch ourselves sooner.

Great counsel can be found in Caroline's apology. Time spent being angry is such a waste. God is cheering us on, ready to forgive us when we fail. He gives us the strength to apologize and ask for forgiveness from those we have hurt. Ultimately, He wants more for us and for our homes—more life, more peace, more grace. When we keep our words and our attitudes under His reign, He gives us so much more.

> May these words of my mouth and this meditation of my heart be pleasing in your sight, LORD, my Rock and my Redeemer.
>
> PSALM 19:14 NIV

Think of a time when you found yourself angry with someone. Now that it's over, does the time and energy you spent seem wasted? Can you feel God's gentle leading to apologize for your words?

36

BMW

"Anyone can have a child; that
doesn't make him a father."
—Charles Ingalls

Not all of us had fathers growing up. Those of us who did knew how much they loved us through their actions. It is one thing to have a biological father, but sometimes it is another to grow up with a loving parent.

Charles Ingalls is one of the most beloved fathers of television history. He inspired a generation of viewers to cherish their children with love, discipline, and grace. In the episode "Someone Please Love Me," he encourages one father to do what every child desires: to spend quality time with a loving parent.

When I was little, I thought "Pa" was my dad, even though we saw him only on the set. After our time on the show ended, I learned what a real dad was from a top-notch example. My stepdad married my mom and, as he liked to say, "three little girls under the age of six." Having been a bachelor for nearly fifteen years, he'd acquired lots of man-toys. An old sports car, a motorcycle, and a catamaran cluttered up the backyard when we moved in. One by one, he sold them all. His new family consumed all his time and money.

Years later, my older sister Michelle asked him how he felt about giving up his hobbies. His response spoke of his sacrifice and deep love for us, children who didn't share his blood or his last name.

"I traded them all for a BMW," he replied.

We gave him a strange look; he drove a van. Then he explained that his BMW was a Brenda, Michelle, Wendi and that it was the best decision he ever made. My stepdad wasn't perfect, but his love backed by action won us over.

With the help of Charles Ingalls, the father reunites with his child and vows to try harder. Fathers are human. They make mistakes and disappoint us. The only dad who won't ever let us down is our heavenly Father. He is the kind of dad we all have dreamed of having—even better than Charles Ingalls.

"Call no man your father on earth, for you have one Father, who is in heaven."

MATTHEW 23:9 ESV

What were the actions of your earthly father that spoke loudest? What do you appreciate most about the perfect love of our heavenly Father?

37

HE COLLECTS
OUR TEARS

"After what you've been through
you have every right to be
afraid, every right to cry."

—MARY INGALLS KENDALL

Traumatic events change us, and triggers from our past cause fear to rise. Shedding tears is often our body's natural reaction. Adam's crossing the river triggered his memory of going blind; one slip on a rock and a concussion had changed everything for him. Hearing the rushing water again stopped him in his tracks, the fear paralyzing. Mary validated Adam's feelings and reminded him his tears spoke of experience, not weakness.

There are some things about brain surgery I won't ever get over. The intense memories will always be with me. The day before I left the hospital, worry consumed me. I didn't know how I would handle the pain without the comfort of my IV. My surgeon suggested I use that day to practice taking my medication orally, giving me a glimpse of the reality ahead.

The first round passed without a hitch. Then, earlier than expected, I felt a prickly sensation on my scalp and a dull headache growing on my brow. Pressing the call button beckoned my nurse into the room. She walked in, holding a white paper cup containing two pills. As I washed them down with a drink, the nurse reminded me of the thirty-minute delay of oral medications.

Panic took over as my body trembled from the pain. Tears flooded my eyes as the throbbing in my head grew worse. The second hand on the wall clock seemed frozen in place. I needed help. My mom and younger sister came to the rescue, just in time. They reminded me that God was with me, encouraged me to trust Him with the unknown. And gave me permission to cry.

Living through life-changing circumstances often is accompanied by moments of fear. The memory is too fresh. We never know when it will hit or what our reaction might be. We hope to conquer the challenges on our own, but like Adam, we can't always defeat them without help from the Lord and the encouragement of a loved one.

God created us to need help—from Him and others. Our tears of fear are not overlooked; He knows what we have endured and who can comfort us.

> When I am afraid, I will put my trust in you. . . . You keep
> track of all my sorrows. You have collected all my tears in
> your bottle.
>
> PSALM 56:3, 8 NLT

Does fear from a past event still haunt you? How can you surrender that experience to God's loving hands? Who can come alongside you?

38

A BOX OF CHOCOLATES

*"If God went to all the trouble to make
a Laura Ingalls, he certainly wouldn't
want her to act like someone else."*

—CAROLINE INGALLS

W hen we dislike our own personalities and mimic others', we
can miss out on God's greatest blessings. People around us
will sometimes be better-looking or have different talents from ours,
but God created each of us to be a one-of-a-kind masterpiece. Envy is
like one piece of art in a museum wishing it were the painting down
the hall; it's impossible.

The "Rivals" episode makes me think of my high school days.
Laura wanted to look older and prettier, like her sister Mary, to attract
the attention of Jimmy Hill. I longed for my sister's athletic ability.
Brenda had volleyball skills I could only dream of. I wanted to be like
her, so I started acting the way she did.

In the process, I lost some of what made me *me*. My mom noticed
the problem and came to my room one day, just as Ma climbed the
ladder to the Ingallses' loft to deliver wise words to Laura.

Mom handed me a box bearing a picture from the movie *Forrest
Gump*. Inside, beautiful little chocolates rested like gems on velvet.
The thin paper covering the pillows of sweetness bore a quote from
Forrest's mother: "Life is like a box of chocolates; you never know
what you're gonna get."

My mom must have learned a thing or two from Caroline Ingalls, because her words gave me hope. She shared how my life would be full of surprises. Some of my chocolate-experiences would be irresistibly wonderful, and others, not so much. And then she told me something surprising.

"In every box of chocolate, you'll find a piece so wonderful that you never dreamed it would be there. I know God has a few of those pieces in your life-box. But the only way to discover them is to be who God created you to be. Be yourself. He can't use you if you act like Brenda."

That day a transformation happened in my mind: I began to embrace who God created me to be. The result? My box of "chocolates" has contained experiences sweeter than I ever imagined. The wisdom of Caroline Ingalls and my mother made all the difference.

We are God's masterpiece. He has created us anew in Christ Jesus, so we can do the good things he planned for us long ago.

EPHESIANS 2:10 NLT

❖ ——————————— ❖

Have you ever tried to act like someone else? Did someone
help you see the work of art God created in you?

39

MORE THAN SUNDAY RITUALS

*"Fellowship and neighborliness
are not just for Sundays."*

—CAROLINE INGALLS

For many believers, Sundays transform our daily activities. Some of us put on our Sunday clothes and Sunday smiles and head to church. Setting our busy schedules aside, we take time to talk to people in the lobby and greet other churchgoers after the opening song. We sing and pray and read from the Bible. Later we sit out on our decks and laugh with our neighbors or go out for Sunday brunch together. Caroline Ingalls noticed the tendency of her children to act differently on Sundays. She gently reminded Laura and Mary that kindness is for every day of the week.

My children don't always get along. Like many siblings, they irritate each other easily. But for some reason, Sundays are a whole different story. I don't know what happens at church to alter their thinking. Almost every weekend after service, they disappear into one of their rooms and have the best time together. More than on any other day!

Sometimes I find myself wishing that Sunday would come around so the bickering would stop for a few glorious minutes. It's such an incredible, Spirit-filled day. And we all need more time to come together and refresh our souls before the week starts.

I realize every day can't be a Sunday, but how can we bring a piece of it into the ordinary days? I'd like to think our patience and kindness are not dependent on the day of the week. My faith has to be more than simple knowledge, more than Sunday rituals.

The fact is, the Holy Spirit is always with us—He never leaves us. If through the Spirit the love of Christ is dwelling within us, then naturally it will spill over into every corner of our lives. We can cultivate this love all the days of the week when we obey and make a special effort to be good to the people around us. Caroline's advice always rings true: kindness is for every day.

I pray that from his glorious, unlimited resources he will empower you with inner strength through his Spirit. Then Christ will make his home in your hearts as you trust in him. Your roots will grow down into God's love and keep you strong.

EPHESIANS 3:16–17 NLT

What do you do differently on Sundays? How can you integrate your faith with your everyday schedule?

40

TRUE RICHES

"You see folks thinking more and more about the wealth
of gold and less and less about the real wealth—
your loved ones, your friends, and even your God."
—CHARLES INGALLS

If we aren't careful and intentional, materialism can shift our focus from what matters most. We'll fall into the trap of thinking the accumulation of possessions can make us happy. When panning for gold cultivates greed in and around him, Charles Ingalls decides to take a loss and leave behind the hopes of striking it rich in the gold country of Shadow Creek. Returning to Walnut Grove empty-handed, he has never felt so good.

My husband and I also gave up an investment. We rushed into buying our first house. The market was high and I'd just returned to work after having our son. We thought owning a home would bring us happiness, not more stress. With a newborn in one arm, I unpacked boxes with the other. I played the role of mom when my son's eyes were open and employee while he slept.

Sometimes we spread ourselves too thin to get what we want. Life has a way of correcting itself. Unfortunate events make us stop and rethink what's important.

In the midst of this busy season, my stepdad died suddenly and I shriveled into a heap on the floor. Panic attacks and nightmares haunted me. Every siren whizzing by sent a jolt of grief through my heart. Beyond overwhelmed, I quit my job and prayed that God would protect my young son as well as the new baby inside of me. The desire for a house of our own wasn't panning out the way we imagined.

Wanting more is a revolving door, a hamster wheel of continual chasing. Possessions and wealth will never make us happy. The world wants us to believe we need more, but the true riches in life are relationships.

The day the house sold marked a new beginning. We cut our losses and moved to a rental in the country. Downsizing and living within our means gave us immediate time and resources.

Loving God and loving people became our new motto. Like Charles Ingalls, we wanted to focus on the real wealth found in relationships. It's been ten years thinking this way, ten years of turning our backs on the desire for more. The house we live in may not be ours, but we are loving every minute. And loving, every minute.

Don't love the world's ways. Don't love the world's goods. Love of the world squeezes out love for the Father. Practically everything that goes on in the world—wanting your own way, wanting everything for yourself, wanting to appear important—has nothing to do with the Father.

1 JOHN 2:15–16 MSG

What do you find yourself wishing for? Does the desire for more possessions pull you away from relationships? What about your relationship with God?

41

THROUGH STORMS AND FALLS

"Blizzards don't stop Charles and Jonathan."
—CAROLINE INGALLS

W hen storms break out, our heavenly Father is ready to protect us. His love never gives up. Caroline feels the same way about Charles and Jonathan's traveling through a blizzard with medicine for the sick townspeople of Walnut Grove. She knows the men will do anything to help their children and neighbors.

Fathers protect their children; it's what they do. On the set of *Little House* with my "Pa," I saw this in action. I was three years old, climbing up into a director's chair during a day of filming. The tall black chair was far too big, and I fell out the back and onto the floor. Michael Landon didn't make a big deal about it, but immediately new little chairs were ordered for us. We were delighted when the chairs arrived with our names printed on the backs. Michael wanted to protect us, but he went beyond simple protection and wowed us with his fatherly love.

God—our good, good Father—wows us all the time. He walks with us through the strongest storms and even the minor falls. Charles and Jonathan pushed through the blizzard and brought medicine and hope to the town. God pushes through all our storms to bring us hope and protection.

Even when I walk through the darkest valley, I will not be afraid, for you are close beside me. Your rod and your staff protect and comfort me.

PSALM 23:4 NLT

Have you ever been protected by a father? What storm has God helped you through? How has God wowed you with His love?

42

HELP NOT ANGER

"People who take advantage of others just demean themselves. They deserve our pity, not our anger."
—Caroline Ingalls

Injustice can get anyone's blood boiling. When we see people treating others poorly, a shockwave of disappointment zings through us. We might immediately jump into action, angry at the perpetrators. When two men humiliate and insult Charles, he gets upset. Caroline is the one to defuse the emotion of the moment, reminding him to be sympathetic, even when empathy or compassion seems undeserved.

A few years ago, I encountered a similar situation. As I walked toward the gates of my children's school after drop-off, I noticed a pack of students waiting just inside the fence. A young boy went running toward the school, bent on getting to class as quickly as possible. The pack filed in behind him and taunted him with mean comments. He kept his eyes on his shoes. As I watched, I could tell it wasn't the first time.

I ran over and caught up with them. The bullying boys dissipated as I followed the student to his classroom, acting as if that's where I was headed. The thought of a child being tormented by his peers sent me marching toward the office, my anger building. I walked through the office door concerned about the boy, unconcerned about protocol.

The school secretary was also troubled, but not vexed. I saw only the emotionally battered little boy. Her focus rested on the mean boys;

she was worried about the reasons they were behaving so badly. She had pity on them and sought to understand. She said something I'll never forget: "People who have been hurt can't help but hurt others."

Unkind people need our help, not our anger. We might be quick to defend the weak without giving a single thought to the abusers who may have also been abused. Only God knows the past experiences that influence their actions. It is not our place to bring judgment on others. Intentionally or not, we all treat people poorly at times.

Purposeful compassion and a mind open to understanding are powerful tools to stop the cycle of hurt people hurting people. Caroline gives us the perfect example to follow. When faced with the choice again, I pray God will give me the wisdom to defend the weak but sympathize with both sides.

> Do not take revenge, my dear friends, but leave room for God's wrath, for it is written: "It is mine to avenge; I will repay," says the Lord.
>
> ROMANS 12:19 NIV

Think of a time when you witnessed someone being mistreated.
Do you find it difficult to have pity on an abuser, to consider
the pain behind their actions? Ask God to help you.

43
_____

CARING FOR
CHILDREN

*"In the meantime, the baby is certainly
in good hands with a new mother."*
—Charles Ingalls

Regardless of our age and whether or not we have brought children into the world, nurturing is often a natural tendency. When Laura and Charles find a baby girl all alone in the middle of nowhere, Laura takes care of the baby as though it were her own. While Charles looks for the infant's mother, the baby is happy and content with Laura.

Babies prefer their mothers over strangers, often becoming upset and agitated with those they don't know. So I've often wondered how my sister and I did so well as eight-month-olds on the set of *Little House,* being held and fed by so many unfamiliar people. My mom told me that it all hinged on Karen Grassle, who played Ma. Just as Charles Ingalls was confident in Laura's abilities, my mother knew we were in good hands with Karen.

Caroline Ingalls's naturally nurturing character was the result of perfect casting. Karen embodied motherly characteristics although she had no prior parenting experience of her own. "Ma" comforted me when I was scared of the camera and somehow convinced us to wear our bonnets, even though we disliked them. She was as giving, wise, and patient as any mother could hope to be.

I've met people like Karen, men and women who love children with authenticity and genuine compassion. I'm blessed to have one of them as my mother-in-law. She loves with an intensity and sacrifice that inspires me to be a better mother.

While we often think of God as our Father, He also displays the nurturing characteristics of a loving mother. Jesus loved children throughout the Gospels, holding them and blessing them. Like Laura caring for an abandoned child, God wraps His arms around us, and He will never let go.

"As a mother comforts her child, so I will comfort you."

ISAIAH 66:13 NRSV

What children has God put in your life to love?
How have you felt God's comforting arms?

44

WELCOME HOME

"Just being home, all of us,
will be picnic enough."
—LAURA INGALLS

Reuniting with our families after a difficult event is a sweet time. Home is where we can be ourselves with the people we love. Laura knew this to be true as she waited for her parents to return home from the hospital with Mary. She longed for the family to be together again.

Leaving the hospital following brain surgery, I couldn't wait to cross the threshold of our home. I missed the faces of my children and my comfortable bed. At the same time, exhaustion and the overwhelming fear of getting back to normal loomed over me. I realized the next eight weeks would be challenging, my brain trying to heal in the midst of chaos. I'd have to make decisions for my children when I couldn't even take a shower unsupervised. I told myself to concentrate on one thing at a time.

The trip home was difficult physically, but I'll never forget walking through the door and seeing my children. Hugs and kisses welcomed me. Flowers filled the house. Smiles and laughter were everywhere. Curiosity won out, and they each took a peek at the long row of metal staples across my scalp. My son decided my incision looked about as awesome as an Orc from *The Lord of the Rings*. We ate and laughed and told stories.

Unfortunate circumstances take us away from our homes and families. When God brings us back together again, it's as wonderful as a family picnic: we are all in one place marveling at what He's done. Laura loved the feeling of her family being whole again. We can too. We can enjoy every moment, sharing the goodness of the Lord and all we've learned.

I will tell of the LORD's unfailing love. I will praise the LORD for all he has done. I will rejoice in his great goodness to Israel, which he has granted according to his mercy and love.

ISAIAH 63:7 NLT

Think of a time when you returned home from something difficult. How did you feel to be with your family again? How did God show you His goodness?

45

SERVING UP JOY

*"You know, Mrs. Ingalls, this working
together—it kinda makes you feel good."*
—WILLIE OLESON

S erving others doesn't always come easily. By nature we are self-centered people; our first concern is generally ourselves. In the episode "Stone Soup," Caroline Ingalls attempts to uproot self-centered thinking and teach the children of Walnut Grove how to serve their teacher—who is also her daughter—Mrs. Wilder. Willie is inspired to help Laura by an ancient story—called Stone Soup— about a soldier who makes soup by rallying people together so that each person contributes a small amount. The entire village pitches in to enjoy a hot meal and the company of others. Though an unlikely candidate, Willie is inspired, and spearheads a project to save Laura's orchard.

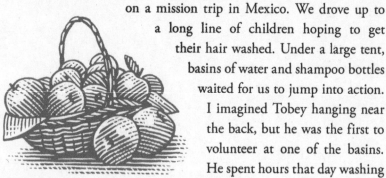

Like Willie, our son Tobey surprised us when we were serving on a mission trip in Mexico. We drove up to a long line of children hoping to get their hair washed. Under a large tent, basins of water and shampoo bottles waited for us to jump into action. I imagined Tobey hanging near the back, but he was the first to volunteer at one of the basins. He spent hours that day washing the heads of little boys he didn't know, spraying and scrubbing dirty scalps. Later that night, as the team gathered together, Tobey said the washday was his favorite part of the trip.

Sometimes all it takes is hearing a story like Stone Soup or finding unexpected joy on a mission trip to teach us to willingly serve others.

Never be lacking in zeal, but keep your spiritual fervor, serving the Lord.

ROMANS 12:11 NIV

What motivates you to serve? How can you help those around you?

46

SISTER SLEEPOVERS

"Sisters are good for telling
your troubles to."
—Mary Ingalls Kendall

The best sisters are around when we need them. Whether we have biological sisters, adopted sisters, or sisters in the Lord, we are blessed by these priceless women. They can tell when our hearts are beaten down. They are ready to hear about our troubles. When Mary finds Laura crying in bed over Almanzo, she takes the time to listen. She gives comfort and advice to soothe Laura's broken spirit.

Having a twin is like inviting your best friend over for an endless sleepover. My mom says Brenda used to climb out of her crib and into mine. Every night was a slumber party for us! When we were young, our experiences were so alike. One word and the other knew what story was coming. No one stood a chance against us in the game of charades. Our faces and mannerisms were so identical that even my mom got confused at times. Sharing the same memories, we understood each other more than anyone else could.

After my brain surgery, Brenda spent the first half of the night with me in ICU. As at a typical sleepover, we didn't get a wink of sleep. We weren't giggling like schoolgirls this time, and she helped me through every dreadful hour. We talked as each morphine bag brought on a new wave of nausea. She rubbed my feet with lotion and gave me sips of cool water as we told stories to pass the time. I would have survived the night without my sister, but God knew her presence would bring a calm and hope I desperately needed.

Sisters are special. They celebrate with us when life is going well and mourn when it takes a turn south. Everyone needs a sister like Mary when trouble hits. God places our sisters in our lives to do what He would do, to love the way He loves, and to stay up all night when we can't face the darkness alone.

A dear friend will love you no matter what, and a family sticks together through all kinds of trouble.

PROVERBS 17:17 TPT

Do you have a sister or brother or friend who shows up for you? How does that person embody God's love? Thank God for a special person in your life.

47

THE STRENGTH
TO ENDURE

*"God does not protect all good people
from misfortune, but what He does
provide is the strength to see His
people through the hard times."*

—REVEREND ALDEN

W hy do we expect God to shield us from trouble? We often
suppose that if people are "good," God will keep problems
and tragedies at bay. But the Bible shows us that our efforts to be good
don't remove hardship. Consider the apostle Paul, who faced ship-
wrecks and beatings and prison. And he was a very good man! God
doesn't take away the hard times, but He does give us the strength to
overcome challenges.

It was the same for the Ingalls family. After a tornado sweeps
through Walnut Grove, Charles is inconsolable. The twister has
destroyed his crops and his hope. He decides to sell the farm and
move back to the Big Woods of Wisconsin. As Charles is praying at
the church one night, Reverend Alden encourages him to seek the
Lord for the fortitude to not give up.

My older sister and her husband had a similar experience, but it
wasn't the words of their pastor that encouraged them—it was furniture. They lived in the South during Hurricane Katrina. Their house

flooded and they lost everything. They began rebuilding, but their hope was running on empty.

Finally their house was nearly done, but the rooms stood bare. My sister visited her church one day to find a semitruck filled with hotel furniture. It had been donated to bless the victims of Katrina. A few truckloads later, my sister's bedrooms were furnished with mattresses, nightstands, and dressers. As my sister looked around at God's wonderful gift, she regained the strength to keep going.

It's startling how wind and water can be so destructive. Whirlwinds of doubt and floods of anger can be just as devastating. Through it all, God comforts us using people and things. For Charles, it was Reverend Alden. And for my sister, a furnished bedroom. When times are tough, open your ears and your eyes to see God's provision. He will give you the strength to endure.

What a wonderful God we have . . . the one who so wonderfully comforts and strengthens us in our hardships and trials.

2 CORINTHIANS 1:3 TLB

Have you ever lived through a natural disaster?
What about a relational or health challenge?
How did God give you strength to continue?

48

WASHING WINDOWS

"My pa always said good hard work on the
land puts the poison out of your system."
—CHARLES INGALLS

C hildren need correction. A child who has not been disciplined creates conflict in the home and steals peace from a family. In Walnut Grove, the Davenports' joy disappears when they discover their visiting grandson is abusive and dishonest. After stealing Charles's watch, the boy faces jail or working off the debt on the Ingalls farm. Hard work can be a great discipline; it transforms an angry heart.

When I was growing up, my parents didn't discipline us by grounding us. Letting us hang out in our rooms for a weekend was too lenient. When we got into trouble, it meant lots of free labor for my folks!

One time during high school, my twin sister and I were supposed to grab a ride home from Disneyland with a family friend. Instead we chose to ride the four hours home with our boyfriends. And . . . we left at midnight.

Boy, were we in a mess of trouble. By the time we strolled in the front door, my mom had quite a list for us. We spent the day washing every window in our house, inside and out. I started out mad, but every clean window revealed more of the truth. My actions were to blame, not my mom's list of chores.

When children realize every act of disobedience results in a consequence, responsibility takes root. The Davenports' grandson Todd works hard with Charles and discovers the source of his anger, resulting in a heart change. Charles was right: putting children to work can be the most effective discipline. Not only do the household chores get done, the children become a joy to be around.

> Discipline your children; you'll be glad you did—they'll turn out delightful to live with.
>
> PROVERBS 29:17 MSG

Did your parents ever discipline you with hard work? How did it affect your perspective? What kind of discipline works best with your children?

49

SIMPLY JESUS

"Happy Birthday, Baby Jesus."

—CARRIE INGALLS

C hristmas brings with it a million things to do. Cooking and wrapping are endless activities. Concentrating on the decorations, the cookies, and the gifts for those I love has often dragged my heart away from the true meaning of the day and from my devotion to the One who has captured my heart. I have become so caught up with the details that I've completely forgotten about the reason we're celebrating.

Preparing for their first Christmas in Walnut Grove, the Ingalls family falls into the same trap. The youngest daughter, Carrie, is the only one who remembers. She spends her one penny on a star for Baby Jesus. She figures it is His birthday, He should have a present under the tree.

We know Christmas is about Jesus and celebrating His humble birth. The greatest gift ever given to the world made salvation possible and love a reality. But I notice many of my December traditions are not about Jesus—they are about me: the parties, the decorating, the baking, and the shopping. We've already received the perfect gift in Jesus, but we ache for more stuff!

I stumbled upon a new gift-giving tradition a few years back. My husband and I wanted to change our family's focus. The new tradition spotlights our simple love for each other rather than receiving every item on our wish list.

Sixteen gifts lie under the tree on Christmas morning, four for each of us. We each ask for something we want, something we need, something to wear, and something to read.

I'm not sure where I heard about the idea, but it has completely taken the chaos out of the season! When we have less to buy, prepare, and wrap, we can center our hearts on the greatest gift of all—like Carrie giving a present to Jesus. We wrap up ourselves and place our hearts under the tree with a tag that reads, To Baby Jesus, Happy Birthday!

The light of God's love shined within us when he sent his matchless Son into the world so that we might live through him.

1 JOHN 4:9 TPT

What Christmas activities fill your December calendar?
Which of your holiday traditions center your thoughts
on Jesus? Which ones might need a new focus?

50

CAREGIVERS
NEED PRAYER

"The worst part about being sick, I think,
is how sad it makes other people."

—LAURA INGALLS

S ickness is difficult, not only for the person with the ailment, but also for the caregivers who are filled with worry. When Laura is suspected of having mountain fever, her parents are beside themselves. Seeing their daughter suffer from her sickness causes them tremendous heartache, and Laura feels bad for her parents. What can we do for people who lovingly care for us yet are filled with distress?

After brain surgery, I had eight weeks of recovery. Some days I made huge strides forward. I'd walk to the mailbox without getting dizzy or find I was able to stand in the shower. But other days I stayed in bed, my head throbbing. I never knew what to expect.

My husband endured the most. The uncertainty of my health drained him, but far worse were my fickle emotions. A coin flip could have decided if I greeted him at the door with a kiss or ignored him completely. The toll my illness took showed on his face, revealing his concern that I might never return to being a healthy and happy person again.

His pain tore me apart. I accepted my own temporary misery and confusion but would have done anything to cheer him up. In the beginning I attempted to fix the problem on my own. I'd force myself to smile, pretending my head didn't hurt. But I couldn't fake it. He saw right through my attempts to mask the pain. The only thing I could do happened to be the best possible option.

Pray.

I prayed for my husband's crushed spirit, for God to be near him in his brokenness. I prayed for Josh to loosen his grip and trust God to take care of me. And I prayed that as God healed my brain, He would heal my husband's heart.

When we are sick, we welcome every prayer for healing and a quick recovery. But our caregivers are hurting too. Charles and Caroline's sadness made Laura's heart ache. Behind every sick patient is a caregiver who also needs our prayers for energy and courage and hope.

> The righteous cry out, and the LORD hears them; he delivers
> them from all their troubles. The LORD is close to the bro-
> kenhearted and saves those who are crushed in spirit.
>
> PSALM 34:17–18 NIV

Think of a time when you saw someone hurting because of your pain. How can you lift up others in prayer even while you suffer? Take a moment to pray for the caregivers you know.

51

COPYCAT LOVE

"That man loves me, and I'm talking to a cat."
—MISS COOPER

T here are times in life when we settle for a lesser kind of love. We
rely on people or things in clear view instead of on the perfect
love that's sometimes hard to see. Miss Cooper recognized the love
of her cat was nothing compared to the love of a man. Toby Noe was
a glimpse of a greater affection than she had ever known. But no
human love can compare to the relentless love of God.

In high school I chased after too many relationships. If I didn't
have a boy by my side, I felt empty. The forever-shaped space
divinely created inside our hearts is something only God can fill.
My attempt to stuff that space with other relationships didn't work
out so well.

Each of those friendships ended while the search for love continued. I finally had to say, "I'm done." My heart couldn't handle any
more breaking. I took a holiday from dating and found my Father
tenderly beckoning me to Himself. People don't have the capacity to
love the way God can.

By definition God is love. He's not a copycat or reflection of a
higher love. His love makes all other versions of love possible. People
and cats might love us, but they will never give us the fulfillment that
comes from a relationship with the Lord. Dive deep into His lavish
gift of love.

"For the mountains may move and the hills disappear, but even then my faithful love for you will remain. My covenant of blessing will never be broken," says the LORD, who has mercy on you.

ISAIAH 54:10 NLT

Have you settled for an inferior version of love? If you haven't experienced the love of God, what is stopping you?

LOVING AGAIN

"Hurting goes away; love, never."
—AUNT KEZIA

Losing someone we love isn't easy. In the beginning the hurting seems as if it will never go away. Laura loses her dog, Jack. She doesn't know how to love again because the loss is so painful. Aunt Kezia knows what loss can do—it shuts the door on a heart begging to be filled. Kezia gives Laura permission to talk about Jack, to remember him every day until the sting subsides.

My sister in-law adopted Kezia's advice without ever watching this episode, and the concept cemented in her heart when her baby boy's heart stopped beating two days before he entered the world. Colton never saw his mother's face, but he has forever changed the way she deals with grief.

When Marie lost Colton, she could have disengaged from life, but instead she climbed into the arms of Jesus. He took her grieving heart and filled it so that love could continue to pour out. Colton is part of our family because of the way Marie remembers and celebrates him. We family members never had the chance to meet him face-to-face, but we will in eternity.

When life is one big hurt, run to Jesus. He will meet you in the pain. He can soothe your heart until it's ready to love again. Aunt Kezia begs Laura to open her heart to a new dog because Bandit needs love just as much as Jack did. Loving goes on and on, forever.

"Come to me, all you who are weary and burdened, and I will give you rest."

MATTHEW 11:28 NIV

———— • ————

How do you remember those you've lost?
How has Jesus helped you love again?

53

YOUNG AT HEART

"You're only as old as you feel."
—CHARLES INGALLS

Charles Ingalls seems forever young, infusing his family with humor and positivity. When Caroline learns she is unable to bear any more children, she begins to feel old and useless. Then Charles restages their courting days and asks her to marry him. Again.

Do you know people like Charles Ingalls, people who don't let age dictate their happiness? Our bodies may be slowly withering, but mentally we can still feel young.

Hersha Parady is the actress who portrayed Alice Garvey. She still attends cast events and has more spunk than most of us kids from the show. Hersha has health challenges, but they never stop her from attending.

A few years ago, when the cast was in South Dakota to meet fans and sign autographs, a helicopter pilot walked into the room. He was a *Little House* fan and wanted to take us for a ride over Mount Rushmore. Hersha's eyes lit up, and I jumped at the chance. Buckling our seatbelts on board the chopper, we chatted nervously. Hersha's words stuck with me: "I might be old, but that doesn't mean I can't have fun."

Age truly is a matter of perspective. Charles Ingalls knew that if we feel young, we are young. Let gratefulness soar, and you will too.

They will still give fruit when they are old. They will be full of life and strength.

*Do you let your age dictate your happiness? How
can you change your perspective to stay young?*

54

NO MORE STRIVING

*"Every day he feels he has to
prove himself, and every day it
gets just a little bit harder."*
—MRS. TYLER

C onstantly proving ourselves is an endless battle. The more we demonstrate our ability to succeed, the higher the expectation becomes. Every day of comparing ourselves with others brings more pressure to perform. It's never enough, we feel—the battle will never be won.

I can relate to Mrs. Tyler's statement about her husband trying to out-chop wood with Charles. I spent most of my life trying to outdo my sister. Being a twin, I shared an identical profile with my best friend and biggest competition. At a very early age, I felt the pressure to succeed at something, anything. I was a good student and a good athlete, but my sister gave the valedictorian speech and received the MVP plaques.

I compared myself to her in every way. I wouldn't recommend that to anyone! Trying to prove yourself is exhausting, and every day it gets harder and more discouraging. After I had brain surgery, God told me, "No more." He had said it before, but I was finally ready to listen. The words rang loud and clear from deep within my heart. They continue to echo every day as a reminder.

No more comparing. No more striving or proving. No more saying you aren't good enough, no more negative talk. You are My precious child, My masterpiece. I made you just the way I planned for the exact purpose that is to come. Trust Me.

Instead of comparing and striving and proving we matter, we can use every gift He's given us, revealing that *God* is the only One who matters. He has orchestrated our lives to accomplish more than we could ever imagine. Mr. Tyler doesn't have to prove himself any longer, and neither do I. God's love has been proven deeper and stronger than all my insecurities.

> Glory be to God, who by his mighty power at work within us
> is able to do far more than we would ever dare to ask or even
> dream of—infinitely beyond our highest prayers, desires,
> thoughts, or hopes.
>
> EPHESIANS 3:20 TLB

How are you striving to prove yourself? Are you tired of trying to live up to others' expectations? What shift can you make so God can use you to accomplish His plans?

55

MEASURING THROUGH MEMORIES

"Where does the time go? It seems like just yesterday."

—LAURA INGALLS WILDER

Looking at the past reveals not just how much we've grown in age, but also in faith. As the Ingalls family gathers around the fire, they share stories of past Christmases. Laura remembers the Christmas snowstorm in the Big Woods and how Mr. Edwards came with gifts for the family. The Ingalls family understands that time goes by fast, but memories stay to remind us of where we've been and how we've grown.

I wasn't stuck in a snowstorm like the Ingalls family, but I did travel down memory lane one Mother's Day weekend. My children and I took a trip to Hume Lake Christian Camp in the Sierra Nevada Mountains—possibly my favorite place on the planet. It's where I met Jesus and where my faith became real.

The first afternoon, I let the kids relax and went for a run around the lake. The scent of hot pine needles mixed with the dusty trail took me back to my first summer there. I looked around at the trees and realized that they had watched me grow up. And they'd grown with me. We had both endured the harsh winters and hot fires of life. Those trees are still growing, still pointing up to the Creator. As I hope I am.

Christmas memories and important moments in our faith story are worth revisiting. Take time to remember all that God has done in you.

"Remember the things I have done in the past. For I alone am God! I am God, and there is none like me."

ISAIAH 46:9 NLT

Think of a place where God has spoken to you.
Relive those memories and thank Him.

56

THE GIFT OF LONELINESS

"You're never alone, Half-Pint. Not ever."
—Charles Ingalls

B eing lonely isn't always about not having people around. Loneliness can hit in a house full of people. In this two-part episode, Laura can't get through to Almanzo. He's had a stroke, leaving his body paralyzed and spirit hopeless. The wall he's built around himself adds to the worry and silence between them. Charles's reminder is not just for Laura, but for all of us. God never leaves us alone.

When I returned home after my brain surgery, family members and friends came to stay with me while Josh and the kids went to work and school. I loved the company and enjoyed every person who came through our front door. But for some reason I still felt alone.

Feelings aren't always trustworthy, and they often alienate us from the people we love. Being misunderstood can make us feel as lonely as a solitary sailor lost on the vast ocean. Who could relate to what I was experiencing? Feelings can deceive us, but in the end, loneliness often draws us closer to Jesus. He was my Navigator, leading the boat back to shore.

If you're feeling lonely the way Laura was, hold on to Jesus. You're truly never alone.

"The time is coming—indeed it's here now—when you will be scattered, each one going his own way, leaving me alone. Yet I am not alone because the Father is with me."

JOHN 16:32 NLT

How has your loneliness brought you closer to Jesus?
How has it made you sensitive to the needs of others?

57

SHADY TACTICS

*"Don't be upset. You ran into the
world's best salesman."*

—Charles Ingalls

A salesman's promises aren't always trustworthy. The backstory may be false, or the item isn't worth the price. In this episode, Caroline Ingalls believes the sad stories of a traveling merchant and trades food for some of his wares. She discovers later that the sad stories weren't true and is upset that she was tricked. Yet the dishonest man gives Mary and Laura an idea to make Reverend Alden's birthday gift even better.

Most of us have experienced something similar. What can we do when people disappoint, deceive, or betray us? Remember that God is always at work. Yes, even then.

My second year of college, I went home for Thanksgiving with plans to return with a new car. My mom and I pulled into a used car lot, our eyes set on a gorgeous white Bronco II with a bright blue stripe across her middle. We circled the vehicle, climbed in the high seats, and marveled at the price.

The salesman sauntered over, taking his sweet time. He told us all about the new rims, paint job, and four-wheel drive tranny. We were sold before he even put the keys in the ignition. I turned the key and the engine sputtered. Again, I tried. Nothing. He shooed me out of the driver's seat and muttered something.

As he turned the key, giving it a bit of gas, the engine roared to life. He continued to baby the pedal until he felt confident with the idle. The words he said next still ring in my ears: "This beauty just needs a little TLC. You think you can give 'er that?"

We bought the car. I named her Sammy and gave her all the TLC I had. A month later, as I was driving home for Christmas, she overheated, and my not-yet-boyfriend and I had to ditch her on the side of the road and pile into a friend's car. The only available seat was Josh's lap. Awkward? You bet.

My dad spent way too much money on Sammy. I ended up selling her for parts a year later. But by then, Josh and I were sweet on each other—and ultimately married. Those memories of being stranded rank high among my unforgettables.

God works in the strangest ways. Caroline and I have experience with talented salesmen, yet somehow it all worked out. God uses even unpleasant experiences to bring people together. Reverend Alden receives a birthday gift and I married a great guy. Sometimes the worst of circumstances and the best of salesmen pave the way to the brightest of futures.

You can make many plans, but the LORD's purpose will prevail.

PROVERBS 19:21 NLT

Have you ever been tricked? Describe a time when a bad decision had positive consequences. How did God use it to accomplish His will?

58

PRICELESS FRIENDS

"Willie, you can't buy friends."
—NELS OLESON

Real friends are hard to find and never bought. Willie Oleson doesn't have any buddies. Even after bribing the other boys with black licorice, he can't convince them to join him in the school play. Nels reminds his son that in order to have true friends, he has to be a friend to others.

I have a priceless friend. We live nine hours apart, so about once a year we meet up for a few days to walk and talk and eat. We save all our best adventures and worst sob stories for our time together.

Six months after my brain surgery, we found ourselves in Santa Barbara for the weekend. The first night we started walking. We covered months of happy stories and sad ones. We passed quaint little homes on tree-lined streets, and then walked a new path back to our room.

As we approached the main street, a huge building lit up by old historic lanterns beckoned us, accompanied by the sweet strum of a guitar. The archway leading to a courtyard garden acted as the sound stage. The area created wondrous echoes. It is one of those unforgettable moments etched in my mind. We didn't say a word; we didn't have to. All our words were spent, tears had fallen, and then the strings of a musician's hand soothed our weary hearts.

The time together always flies by faster than a perfect summer day, but the fullness my heart feels as I drive away lingers for months. The time isn't just relaxing, it's healing. I'm strengthened to return home where I can love my husband and my children better than I could before. My friend and I motivate each other to be the best versions of ourselves, honoring the Lord as we each walk our unique path.

Deep friendship is a gift from God. When life goes a little sour, He puts people in our lives to sweeten up the hardest of seasons. True friends know us in the deepest parts and still love us. This world wouldn't be nearly as fun without friends to share it. Real friends can't be bought, but they are definitely worth every piece of black licorice in the world.

> Sweet friendships refresh the soul and awaken our hearts with joy, for good friends are like the anointing oil that yields the fragrant incense of God's presence.
>
> PROVERBS 27:9 TPT

Do you have a friend who walks with you through life? Can you be a friend to someone looking for encouragement?

59

TRADITIONS

*"I don't want to discourage you, but my recipe was
handed down from generation to generation."*
—MRS. OLESON

E very family passes down a recipe or tradition, something that is
repeated over and over. It can be as simple as Saturday morning
blueberry pancakes or as elaborate as an authentic Chinese dinner,
which my father-in-law prepares on New Year's Eve.

Mrs. Oleson was sure her famous family recipe would win
the pie contest, and Caroline hoped hers would. But little old
Mrs. Grandie's pumpkin pie stole the judge's

taste buds. Her recipe had obviously been around a long
time and Reverend Alden
couldn't help but present
her with a blue ribbon.

When I was growing
up, I loved rice pudding.
The recipe came from my
Grandma Lou, who used
to make it whenever we
stayed at her house. Some

of my fondest memories revolve around long days of swimming in her
pool and having rice pudding for supper.

My stepdad never considered rice pudding a sufficient main course, so my mom put a twist on the tradition: she made it only on rainy afternoons. Coming home after a drippy school day and gathering around the simmering pot of creamy rice is a favorite memory. I have continued the same tradition with my children.

Traditions hold special meaning for us, and we want them to become part of the legacy for future generations. While I'll never forget the smells of cinnamon while the rain drizzled outside, I hope to leave my children with more than a few simple recipes.

To start a tradition, all it takes is doing something once. And then repeating it again and again until you wouldn't want it any other way.

It turns out lots of people have never tasted rice pudding. One day I picked up my neighbors' kids after school when the forecast changed to rain. We shared our family tradition with them; it may not have been as tasty as Mrs. Oleson's pie, but it came close. Now when the gutters begin to trickle and I gather my measuring cups, there's just one last thing to do—double the recipe. Sharing is a tradition worth repeating!

He issued his laws to Jacob; he gave his instructions to Israel. He commanded our ancestors to teach them to their children, so the next generation might know them—even the children not yet born—and they in turn will teach their own children.

PSALM 78:5–6 NLT

＊━━━━━━━━━━━ ＊ ━━━━━━━━━━＊

What is your favorite family recipe? How can you
share it with those outside your family? What do
you want to pass on to future generations?

6 0

WORTHLESS WORRYING

*"I wonder how much of our lives are spent worrying
about things that just don't mean anything."*

—CHARLES INGALLS

S enseless worrying is often interrupted by real heartache. Sorrow over unthinkable events puts our meaningless inconveniences in perspective. When Mary goes blind, Charles Ingalls realizes how much time he spent worrying about silly problems. Tragedy has a way of correcting the lens, but God tells us that worrying does no good.

A few years ago, my lens was corrected in an instant. It was a super-busy day I spent speeding from one appointment to the next. At the dentist with my kids, I answered emails and made a grocery list. Maybe if I wrote it all down I wouldn't forget anything.

Jetting out the door with new toothbrushes in hand, we raced down the speedway to soccer practice. I felt the heavy weight of trying to hold it all together, worried about everything. At the grocery store, the carts were as numerous as ants raiding a picnic, a common occurrence at 5:30 on a school night. I managed to get out of there and back to the field with two minutes to spare. The coach was waiting. I guess practice had ended a little early.

Getting home didn't solve a thing. Homework still needed to be done, and dinner was one big question mark. I'd forgotten the pasta sauce for the leftover noodles. Great, now what are we going to eat?

Josh walked through the door. He gave me a hug and asked about my day. I started complaining about minor details, trivial worries that didn't matter. He listened, and when I finished, he gave me another hug, leaning in tight.

"Did you hear what happened today? Another shooting at a school."

I didn't know what to say. I walked out onto the deck for a breath of fresh air. The problems of my day paled in comparison to what some parents were dealing with. Silence replaced my insignificant worries.

In his sadness over Mary's blindness, Charles experienced a flash of insight. Worrying about unimportant things is a waste. Whether our troubles are big or small, worrying doesn't solve anything. Ralph Waldo Emerson is credited with saying, "Sorrow looks back. Worry looks around. Faith looks up."

"Who of you by worrying can add a single hour to your life? Since you cannot do this very little thing, why do you worry about the rest?"

LUKE 12:25–26 NIV

What insignificant things do you worry about? How does real tragedy change your perspective? When you are tempted to worry, how can you look up?

61

WHO TOLD YOU THAT?

"My advice to you is, don't listen."
—CHARLES INGALLS

We hear statements about ourselves every day, positive and negative. Words are powerful and unfortunately, the negative things we hear tend to stay with us longer than the good ones do. After school one day, Nellie tells Laura her pa is a scaredy-cat for not signing up to fight the boxing champion. When Laura talks to her father later that night, he tells Laura to cover her ears when she's around Nellie. Nellie is not a trustworthy source, and believing her lies will lead only to trouble.

We have a tendency to believe what we hear without considering the source. The most powerful lies are the ones we speak about ourselves. I've collected my own set based on random statements and my own assumptions. But assumptions are rarely true. They are simply theories in desperate need of confirmation.

Satan is the master of deception. He disguises himself as doubt, even humility at times. He's tricky, masking a lie with an ounce of truth to make me believe all of it. The lies he's been whispering blare with intensity and infuse fear into everything I do.

I'm not smart enough.

I'm not brave enough.

I'm going to fail.

I'm going to make a fool of myself.

God can't possibly use me.

I have to stop and ask who is the source of these ideas. They didn't come from God, and He is the only One who has the authority to tell me who I am, and what I can or can't do. Testing a lie with a simple question reveals who said it.

Asking, "Who told you that?" has transformed the way I live. When faced with a belief about myself, I ask the question. If the words come from Scripture or from time spent in His presence, I accept it as truth. Statements from the world or the devil are critical and filled with self-doubt.

God has told us who we are, and how much He loves us. It's time to start believing God. God's Word rings louder and truer than any lie. He calls us dearly loved, His saints, and His messengers. We are children of light shining amid the darkness. We are conquerors with a heavenly calling designed for good works. We are chosen and coheirs with Christ. The messages of the world are deafening, but as Charles said, the best way to handle it is "Don't listen."

We capture, like prisoners of war, every thought and insist that it bow in obedience to the Anointed One.

2 CORINTHIANS 10:5 TPT

What are the lies you believe about yourself? Who is the author of those lies? What does God's Word say about you?

6 2

TAKE A STAND

*"When you believe in something, you have
to be courageous enough to say, 'This is
what I stand for,' and then patient enough
to let them think about it for a while."*

—Caroline Ingalls

It takes courage to advocate for yourself or someone who needs help. No matter what culture we live in, some people are not respected or valued as they should be. Change starts with one person taking a stand against inequality, giving his or her time and energy to empower a group of people robbed of dignity.

In Walnut Grove, Caroline takes a stand to obtain land rights for women. As a way to protest she stays at the hotel in town and leaves Charles at home to cook and care for the family. Her bravery forces her husband to think about signing the petition. It is a bold stance for the late 1800s, but her actions start a movement of progress that strengthens her community.

Like Caroline Ingalls, my friend Rebecca Snavely has taken courageous steps to defend women in the Democratic Republic of Congo. She is cofounder and executive director of Action Kivu, a nonprofit organization that invests in women and children affected by violence through vocational training and education.

Rebecca was moved to action when she heard about women who lacked education or opportunities for employment. Caroline feels the same way when she learns that women can't own property. Her courage ignites a spark in the other women of Walnut Grove, and the men eventually sign the petition.

God asks us to take a stand for those who can't stand alone, help children who need role models, and give to the poor in our neighborhoods and the world. Caroline Ingalls took a stand, and we can too.

> Defend the defenseless, the fatherless and the forgotten, the disenfranchised and the destitute. Your duty is to deliver the poor and the powerless; liberate them from the grasp of the wicked.
>
> PSALM 82:3–4 TPT

When you think of people in need, who comes to mind? How can you take a stand, however small, to offer your support?

63

RESTING IN GOD'S PROVISION

"You think we'll ever see the day we aren't fretting about money?"
—CHARLES INGALLS

The Ingalls family is a lot like my family. We aren't poor, but every time the bankbook is looking good, something comes up to empty it. New tires for the car and braces for crooked teeth never happen when it's convenient. Charles's job at the mill is slowing down, and his growing children need bigger clothes. He thinks about taking a railroad job, but Caroline doesn't want him to be away from the family that long.

Worrying about money is normal in our society. It may feel as though we can never get ahead without an unexpected expense draining our wallets. My husband often tells me that we are right where God wants us—not rich, but definitely not poor.

Depending on the Lord for every bill to be paid strengthens our trust and deepens our love for the One who provides. Caroline's response is right. She reminds Charles that most folks are just like them, working hard and sometimes coming up short. But our God always comes through. Let's not forget to praise Him every day for His provision.

May my satisfaction be found in you. Don't let me be so rich that I don't need you or so poor that I have to resort to dishonesty just to make ends meet. Then my life will never detract from bringing glory to your name.

PROVERBS 30:9 TPT

What unexpected expenses have come up for you lately? How can you rely on God to provide? Have you thanked Him already for provision on the way?

64

WINNING COMES
AT A PRICE

*"I hope being right is enough for you, because
you're sure paying a high price for it."*
—CAROLINE INGALLS

I can be relentless in an argument. When an idea is firmly planted in my head, I have a hard time relinquishing it. My poor husband has been on the opposite side of far too many "discussions" where I was set on proving my point. These conversations rarely end the way I think they will.

Alice Garvey is a lot like me. She's stubborn and strong-willed. Her job at the post office is a good idea. An even better idea would have been to talk to her husband, Jonathan, about it first. Most of the time Alice and I are right: our reasoning *does* line up. But the problem is that we care more about winning the argument than winning our husbands over.

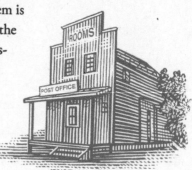

Arguing to win doesn't bring us together; it pulls us apart. Exchanging different opinions opens our eyes to the possibility that maybe both perspectives can pump water, if only we could humble ourselves when the talking begins.

Jonathan doesn't want his wife to work. In his mind, Alice's providing their income makes him feel like less of a man. We all haul around a wagon-full of opinions that mold our interactions. The goal of understanding each other versus winning is much more beneficial. Foolish bickering will lead only to more bickering. Let's fight for the relationships in our lives, even if it means losing arguments now and then.

Most arguments are similar to the Garvey's. We hear words that were never said. Jonathan feels like a failure, and Alice's taking a job confirmed his feelings. Caroline always seems to know what to say. Being right is never worth the price of a happy family.

> Remind everyone about these things, and command them in God's presence to stop fighting over words. Such arguments are useless, and they can ruin those who hear them.
>
> 2 TIMOTHY 2:14 NLT

Do you fight to win? How could you enter an argument with understanding as the goal? Are there any relationships that need healing because of past arguments gone wrong?

65

GOD KNOWS WHAT HE'S DOING

"I can only tell you that there's a reason,
Charles. Believe me, God must have chosen
Mary for some very special purpose."
—REVEREND ALDEN

Trials happen every day, to us and to those we love. We find ourselves in the middle of a dusty road, looking for a drink and an explanation. Adversity reveals weakness we never realized we possess. Most people do what they can to help us, but there are always a few who see our challenges in a different light. These people notice God working and believe that eventually He will make sense of the pain. It's not anything we could perceive in our current state of questioning.

When Mary goes blind, Charles wants to know why. It's Reverend Alden who reminds him that God has a reason. The minister believes in God's plan, but the waiting is difficult. During the worst of times, the Lord strengthens us and molds us into the people He wants us to be. He couldn't have used us in the same way without our time of heartache. God knows what He is doing.

After my brain surgery, a friend came for a visit. I'll never forget what she told me that day. Her voice had a strange energy, one that made me long for the blessing she bestowed.

"I knew God was up to something when I heard about your tumor. He's going to use this for good. You just wait and see."

I shrugged my shoulders and hoped she was right.

Just like Reverend Alden, my friend urged me to be patient. She said my weakness would eventually become my greatest strength. Mary's blindness paved the way to becoming a teacher and to marrying Adam. Writing about my brain surgery experience led me to becoming an author. And for both of us, our worst experience was transformed into wonderful things God planned.

Each time he said, "My grace is all you need. My power works
best in weakness." So now I am glad to boast about my weak-
nesses, so that the power of Christ can work through me.

2 CORINTHIANS 12:9 NLT

*Who has encouraged you to be patient while you
wait for God's purpose to unfold? How has God
used your weakness to bring Him glory?*

66

GOOD, BETTER, BEST

*"It's not a matter of right and wrong; it's a matter
of folks loving and wanting what's best."*
—CAROLINE INGALLS

Good parents make decisions based on love. Charles Ingalls wouldn't let Almanzo marry Laura, not yet anyway. Love was his motive, not control. Laura was upset with her pa, and Caroline lovingly encouraged Charles to keep doing what he thought was best. He believed waiting until his daughter was older would be better.

My mother acted in much the same way after the show ended. *Little House* was a dream job, one we especially appreciated after later pounding the sidewalks of Hollywood for work. We survived two auditions and one commercial before calling it quits.

We made our first mistake when we didn't recognize Ronald McDonald. The McDonald's commercial would have been great exposure, but we had never eaten there. When the producer showed us a picture of Mr. McDonald, we saw nothing more than a man in a red wig and bright yellow overalls. Obviously our agent didn't receive a call-back for that job.

Not long after, we filmed our first commercial, but my mom had second thoughts about continuing our acting careers. The people we were working with after *Little House* didn't know our names. They didn't care if we were tired or hungry. Mom decided we would graduate from acting and pursue kindergarten.

God redirects our paths. He loves us and knows where we should be headed. As Caroline said, it's not about right and wrong, but what's good, better, and best. My mom knew moving on would be best, and it was.

> We know that for those who love God all things work together for good, for those who are called according to his purpose.
>
> ROMANS 8:28 ESV

When has God redirected your path? Do you trust Him to know what is best?

67

WHY SO MUCH?

*"Sometimes I wonder if people know
when they have enough."*

—Caroline Ingalls

Traveling to other countries, I've realized I have more than I need. *Enough* is a slippery word; it's impossible to grasp with the standard constantly changing. For the Ingalls family, finding a few ounces of gold evolves into wanting more than what they need. Caroline is the first to notice what greed can do.

If we reach our current hopes of success, we raise the expectation for the future. Our prior *enough* is no longer sufficient.

A few summers ago, I boarded a plane for Costa Rica. After four years of volunteering with high schoolers, I was one of the chaperones for the senior youth group trip. Our overflowing bags packed with all the makings of a summer camp, we were bound for the Bribri Indians deep in the mountains of Talamanca.

Camp was fabulous. The graduated seniors led crafts and games and an obstacle course through the jungle. Mud reached to their waists. Our camp host, Hugo, led an endless dance party one night. The gospel stirred in souls searching for hope, and we celebrated as fourteen new believers were baptized in the river. Our time with the Bribri Indians changed us. We learned to give of ourselves freely.

With camp over, we began our preparations for an overnight

trip to a small village deep in the jungle. We didn't need much—just enough for one night in a community called Katsi.

As I hoisted my pack, I couldn't believe the weight of my load. I'd stuffed in one thing after another, just in case. But just-in-case extras accumulate fast. After a truck ride, a river crossing, and two bus trips, we arrived dripping with perspiration. Our guide, Hugo, swung his bag—about the size of a preschooler's backpack—over his shoulder. His eyes danced with energy as he glanced down at my stuff.

"Why so much? You need all these things?"

I stared out the open-air windows. I felt sticky and very rich. Not a good rich. I had more than enough, and it was weighing me down. The luxuries I carried were unneeded frills these people had never known.

We often desire comfort within arm's length. The more comfortable we are, the heavier our packs become. Caroline noticed when enough was enough. Do we?

> He who loves money will never have enough money to make him happy. It is the same for the one who loves to get many things. This also is for nothing.
>
> ECCLESIASTES 5:10 NLV

Do you know someone who travels lightly? How does he or she inspire you to live? Can you think of a way you can travel a little lighter?

68

EMBRACE FORGIVENESS

"I don't know what's wrong with me.
I've become so mean. It just doesn't feel
right to be mean, to even Sam."
—HESTER SUE TERHUNE

When people hurt us, deep down we often turn our backs on them, calloused to the relationship. Hester Sue has been turning her back until her ex-husband comes to Walnut Grove. She hasn't forgiven him for the years of drinking and gambling that destroyed their marriage, but Sam wins the approval of the town with his generosity and good manners. The battle rages within Hester Sue: How do you forgive and show kindness to someone who doesn't deserve it?

I've been in Hester Sue's shoes before—in a relationship with more broken promises and disappointment than I dare to remember. I tried being angry and mean, but those things didn't help the hurt inside.

It wasn't until I began to understand the forgiveness of God that I could forgive the one who hurt me. Forgiving doesn't mean putting ourselves back in harmful relationships, but living with an unforgiving heart makes kindness almost impossible. And it feels so wrong to be mean, doesn't it?

Follow Hester Sue's lead and embrace forgiveness. You'll feel better on the inside with kindness flowing out of you.

Be kind and compassionate to one another, forgiving each
other, just as in Christ God forgave you.

EPHESIANS 4:32 NIV

*Is it possible to be kind with an unforgiving heart? Who do you
need to extend forgiveness to, whether it's deserved or not?*

69

KEEP RUNNING!

*"No sir, I'm not going to give up. Everyone has
problems once and again. You can't let that stop you."*

—LAURA INGALLS

Perseverance focuses on the future, not on the heartache of the past. When a tornado moves through Walnut Grove, it destroys Laura's home. She doesn't realize the extent of the damage because

a tree limb knocks her unconscious as she is rescuing a cat. Recovering at her parents' house, Laura has plenty of reasons to dwell on the past. After a few days, Laura is ready to see the house and takes Baby Grace along with her.

This episode is one of the few we vividly remember filming, and I love the lesson it teaches. It reveals our human nature when we let current circumstances dictate our happiness. Laura has just told Baby Grace how she won't give up—and then they come upon the demolished house. She is furious and begins throwing boards into the already broken windows. At that moment, afraid of her sister's anger, Grace turns around and runs.

When we were filming this scene, Michael told us to keep running until we were out of frame. Baby Grace didn't know exactly what "out of frame" meant, but we did the scene perfectly. As the camera rolled, Michael yelled over and over again, "Keep running! Don't look back!"

I imagine God saying something similar, encouraging us to persevere, with our eyes focused on our future hope, not on the mistakes or damaging events of our past. Looking back at disaster only makes us angry and sad, like Laura seeing her home dismantled into a pile of twisted lumber. It wasn't an easy road for Laura and Almanzo, but they didn't give up. Persevering and focusing on the future, they eventually built a new home filled with happiness.

Keep running and don't look back.

I am still not all I should be, but I am bringing all my energies to bear on this one thing: Forgetting the past and looking forward to what lies ahead.

PHILIPPIANS 3:13 TLB

*How can you persevere by forgetting the hurt
of the past and focusing on the future?*

70

HARDSHIP BRINGS WISDOM

"He's a special little guy."

—CHARLES INGALLS

When Solomon Henry, a runaway kid, starts talking at the dinner table, the Ingalls family stops to listen. They're shocked when he offers to sell himself to them as a slave so he can go to school and learn to read. He wants to succeed in the future and thinks this is the only way. Solomon closes his eyes and tells the family about how he dreams of learning to write his name. Doesn't everyone deserve a chance to learn?

Children often surprise us with the things they say. A child sometimes speaks with such wisdom and grace we are moved to the cores of our souls. Children who have endured extreme challenges often share profound insights.

My nephew Cody has had open-heart surgery. He's six. His short life has been full of unexpected medical problems. It started when he and his twin brother arrived twelve weeks early and tiny. He spent almost three months in the NICU before going home connected to an oxygen tank. One afternoon Cody was unresponsive. A terrifying ambulance ride led to an even more terrifying coma. After days of worry, we all feared the worst was ahead.

But God opened Cody's eyes and protected his body. Cody is—as Solomon Henry was—a special little guy. He's in tune with details most kids miss, more reflective than any child I've met.

A few summers ago, we headed to Texas for a visit with Cody, his twin, Tucker, and the rest of the family. My children met their little cousins and experienced life on a houseboat. Cody and Tucker are walking miracles. Though they're small in stature, their huge hearts are full of inspiration.

The first day, Cody tripped going up to the top deck of the houseboat and cut his top lip. It looked terrible. My sister dried his tears and got him an ice pack. Cody suffered through the rest of the day with his lip big and bruised.

The next morning we settled on the front porch, eating French toast and strawberries. Cody snuggled up next to my sister. He let out a deep sigh, his lip still swollen. "This is the most perfect day." His eyes drifted over the water, completely at peace.

The moment, like our syrup-drenched toast, oozed gratitude. I've never experienced such thankfulness overflowing from a little heart when life was far from perfect.

People who have endured much have much to share. Solomon Henry and my nephew Cody are worth listening to. Regardless of their age, they challenge us to be grateful. Solomon's words make Laura realize how much she takes her education for granted, and he inspires her to work hard and be thankful. God's plan for us is always a thankful heart, even in the midst of trouble and fat lips.

Let joy be your continual feast. Make your life a prayer. And in the midst of everything be always giving thanks, for this is God's perfect plan for you in Christ Jesus.

1 THESSALONIANS 5:16–18 TPT

When have you heard wisdom from the mouth of a child? How do you explain that many people who have lived through hardship still possess gratitude?

71

DELAYED DREAMS

"It's a dream I made myself forget,
and now it's coming true."

—CAROLINE INGALLS

O ccasionally we are forced to let dreams go. Caroline Ingalls dreamed of seeing her daughter become a teacher. Mary's blindness robbed her of that dream, but only for a short while.

When my doctor discovered my brain tumor, I was in the middle of training for a half marathon. After the shock wore off, I asked my neurosurgeon one simple question: "What about my race? Can I still run?"

His eyes grew big, surprised that I could even lace up my trainers. He shook his head and put me on immediate activity restriction. I wasn't allowed to walk to the mailbox.

It's not that I'm a great runner. I'm not fast, and sometimes I'd rather stop and walk. But when I decide to do something, I'm all in. I made a promise to myself that day. *Next year I'm running the Monterey Bay Half Marathon. No matter what.*

Three months later, at my first follow-up appointment, I asked if I could start running. My surgeon chuckled and then realized I was serious.

"A year from now, if you're lucky. But even then, you may not ever be able to run like you did before."

My heart sank, but it gave me greater resolve to prove him wrong.

The time went by quickly as I attempted to master the coordination and balance I'd lost. After my first run, a year after my surgery date, I almost gave up. I looked as out-of-sorts as a blind Mary making her way down a busy street. My brain didn't know how to integrate so many moving parts. The road to recovery would be a long, hard journey.

Two years and eight days after the original race, I ran 13.1 miles along the ocean in Monterey, never stopping even to take a picture. I ran across the finish line in the best shape of my life and with a smile on my face.

Sometimes the wait is longer, and the road is harder than we ever imagined. Preparation and diligent training seem wasted because of an unforeseen event. Caroline never thought she'd see her daughter teach, but God made it possible. He placed Mary in the middle of a school full of blind children needing instruction.

Never give up, and never stop running after your dreams.

This is the reason we do not give up. Our human body is wearing out. But our spirits are getting stronger every day.

2 CORINTHIANS 4:16 NLV

What dream have you been forced to set aside? Does the road to achieving it seem too long or too hard? How can you take a step toward your dream?

72

POP YOUR BUBBLE

"They may not read the same Bible as
we do or worship God in the same way,
but they are His children too."
—CHARLES INGALLS

P eople have a tendency to choose what is familiar. To our detri-
ment, we exclude people because their beliefs don't line up with
ours. When a Native American tribe passes through Walnut Grove,
the townspeople become hostile. Charles Ingalls and a few others help
the visitors escape.

I grew up in a small, middle-class town where almost everyone is
related. I went to a big church down the street from the public high
school. Sunday services, church choir, and youth group filled my weekly
activity schedule. I lived in a proverbial and very comfortable bubble.

Going away to college didn't change that. A similar Christian
bubble overflowed with people who believed the same things I did.
Maybe their race or color didn't match mine, but our hearts beat for
the same things.

It wasn't until years later that my bubble burst. I landed my first
full-time job as an administrative assistant in a small company. I stuck
out like a Native American riding through Walnut Grove. I was living
the words "Go into all the world" (Mark 16:15).

I came in contact with all kinds of lovely people. I met some who
believed in things I'd never heard of and others who didn't believe

in anything but themselves. I couldn't change them, but I could respect them.

With the heart of Charles Ingalls, I didn't let their differing views ruin our relationships. My coworkers knew I went to church. I think they found it refreshing that I didn't debate hot topics or invite them to every outreach event. I lived my life and they lived theirs. With respect.

Years later, after I'd long left that job, a former coworker sent me a message. She said Jesus had changed her life, and I had a part in showing her the way. Not by the words I said, but by respecting the space she needed to find her way to God.

Respect for others' beliefs starts with valuing every person with whom we come in contact. God made each one of us, and He calls us to honor all people everywhere. Charles Ingalls gave every person a chance, no matter his or her appearance or beliefs. We can pop our bubbles and do the same.

> Treat everyone you meet with dignity. Love your spiritual
> family. Revere God. Respect the government.
> 1 PETER 2:17 MSG

Do you live in a Christian bubble? Think of one
way you can break out of it. How can you respect
those who don't believe what you do?

73

ROLE MODELS

*"I can believe in all those heroes, like Washington,
Lewis and Clark, and Buffalo Bill. I mean, they
did big things, and I wish I could be like them."*
—WILLIE OLESON

Role models inspire young people and are often found in the most unlikely places. Willie found his heroes in a fictional magazine about settlers moving west. While most of the content he read wasn't exactly educational, it set his sights on achieving greater aspirations.

When I was growing up, our family hosted a foreign exchange student from Japan. We got to know some of her friends, one young man in particular. He was fascinated to hear about my time on *Little House*. Charles Ingalls was his role model. Overwhelmed by Pa's love and concern for his children, the student wanted to emulate Charles Ingalls when he became a father. He shared that in Japan, fathers don't usually show emotion. They don't say "I love you," and they rarely hug their children. It's not surprising that a television star became his hero.

We see God in creation and His Word, but He also moves through various methods to inspire new courses of action and belief. Our society learns from entertainment, and God uses whatever He can to guide us. Willie's heroes fought in the Wild West. What do yours do?

Follow my example, as I follow the example of Christ.

1 CORINTHIANS 11:1 NIV

Who is your role model and why? How is
God revealing Himself to you?

74

THE YOUNG CARETAKER

"You've taken care of me all your life, Pa.
Now it's my turn to take care of you."
—TIMOTHY FARRELL

Timothy Farrell gladly quit school to care for his sick father. Then he spent his days stealing eggs from the hen house and pies from Caroline's windowsill, and everyone else's in town. He figured his pa had provided for him, now it was his turn. His motives were more respectable than his methods.

When I was a child, I took care of my mom after her emergency appendectomy. My job was to bring her water or a snack, maybe a book if she was tired of watching television. While a child taking care of a parent feels backward, children are often more capable than we realize. The responsibility of providing for another can be a giant leap toward increased compassion and maturity.

After brain surgery, my children got a crash course in caretaking. They knew how much water I needed to take my medication and which ice packs were my favorites. All the practice paid off ten months later when my tooth started hurting one Friday night.

On Monday I finally headed to the dentist, who then sent me down the road for a more-than-necessary root canal. The doctor claimed it would be painless, but the two hours of drilling triggered anxiety. Pain and anxiety are not the best companions, so I left the office in a full-fledged panic attack.

I reached our front door in a mess of tears. Josh was out getting my pain medication, but the kids were home. Raegan and Tobey led me to the couch. In an instant, my son had an ice pack and my daughter sat next to me, stroking my head. They rose to the occasion, just like Timothy . . . minus the stealing.

We sometimes shield our children from hard or uncomfortable situations, never wanting them to see us weak. But you know what? They can handle it. Our kids almost always surprise us with their compassionate hearts. Let the young people in your life see you in pain, give them the opportunity to serve you, and maybe tell the neighbors to lock up their chicken coop.

> If they have children or grandchildren, these are the ones
> who should take the responsibility, for kindness should begin
> at home, supporting needy parents. This is something that
> pleases God very much.
>
> 1 TIMOTHY 5:4 TLB

As a child, did you ever take care of your
parents? How have you given the young people
in your life a chance to take care of you?

75

KEEP WALKING

*"You gotta hold the memory of the one you
love and try to make them proud."*

—JONATHAN GARVEY

G rief has many faces. We each process the loss of a loved one
differently. Some of us move on quickly, and others never move
forward at all. The key is to walk boldly into the future. As we reflect
on past memories, inspiration moves us to action. When Jonathan
Garvey's wife dies in a fire, he gets stuck in the past. Grief paralyzes
him. But then Jonathan shifts his focus from inward thinking to out-
ward living. Honoring the one we love motivates every stride toward
the future.

My husband recently agreed to coach a team. It's not the most ideal
situation. The former coach passed away, and my husband is there to
sweep up the pieces of grief and help a group of high school girls play
soccer again. It's not going to be easy to navigate the emotions.

Stepping out onto the field, the team will likely be flooded with
thoughts of the time they spent with their former coach. When the
girls lost their coach, my husband lost a friend. Moving forward can
seem impossible at times. My husband wants to give the players space
to grieve and inspire them to play in a way that will honor the coach's
memory.

It takes courage to keep walking, to keep playing after death has
taken its toll on our hearts. Jonathan discovers the only hope toward

healing for himself and his son is to take a step forward. When we trust in the Lord, He gives us the strength to continue. Overcoming our grief and stepping bravely into the future will make our loved ones proud.

Those who trust in the LORD will find new strength. They will soar high on wings like eagles. They will run and not grow weary. They will walk and not faint.

ISAIAH 40:31 NLT

Have you found it difficult to move on when you are grieving? Give yourself some time; then decide how your life can honor your loved one.

76

MORE THAN JOKES

*"You made me realize I've got something
to say to people. Not just jokes and acting
silly and all, but real things."*
—HARV MILLER

Outgoing personalities are often the center of attention, but these talkative, lighthearted people can have important things to say. Almanzo's friend Harv is a jokester until he meets Eliza Jane. She wants to know the real Harv Miller, not the clown persona behind which he has hidden himself.

Our cast clown was definitely Alison Arngrim, who played Nellie. Today she is a stand-up comedian, with more stories than all the gumdrops in the mercantile. Her Nellie wig and sour frown are crowd-pleasers on her Nasty Nellie Oleson Tour. But if you come to know Alison, you'll learn what she is truly passionate about.

Alison became an activist after her friend and *Little House* husband, Steve Tracy, passed away of HIV/AIDS. She volunteers with AIDS Project Los Angeles and other groups, speaking, teaching, and raising support for those affected by the disease. Alison's other passion is speaking out against child abuse with Protect.org.

Harv realized his heartfelt concerns were more important than joking around. And Alison has seen God use people—even Nellie Oleson—to speak up for others. Do the people around you get to see what you are really passionate about?

Speak up for the poor and helpless, and see that they get justice.

PROVERBS 31:9 NLT

————————•————————

Are you a jokester or quiet? How can you use your unique personality to advocate for others?

77

CELEBRATING
FOR OTHERS

"Why is it, Alice, some folks want and others get?"
—JONATHAN GARVEY

E nvy strips us of all joy. When we want what we don't have, envy is bound to affect our relationships. If we're honest, we feel as though everyone else *gets*—while we sit wanting what we won't ever have. The envy we experience outlasts our friend's new car or vacation in the Caribbean. It's a pointless act of ingratitude.

When Charles Ingalls receives word of an inheritance from a long-lost uncle, Jonathan is envious. He's upset that his family is always wishing for things out of their reach. Jonathan's envy goes too far, and he lets his selfish feelings affect the relationship with his friend Charles. Bitterness can damage a friendship.

I can identify with Jonathan. At one point in my family's life it seemed as if everyone around us was moving into beautiful new homes, driving expensive cars, and traveling to extravagant destinations. We acted as if we didn't want what our friends had. But soon the truth rose to the surface. I had to make a choice: be envious of our friends or celebrate with them.

We celebrated when friends moved into a gorgeous home. Our families got to know each other in Mexico on a missions trip. After my brain surgery, they were a great source of support for us.

Our friends had bought an old house, stripped it down to nothing, and rebuilt it into something absolutely breathtaking. Not once did I feel envious; instead I felt grateful for their friendship and love.

Envy is the beginning of greed and spite. Celebrating is the only good option. It's not always easy, but I've seen how jealousy can destroy a friendship.

Jonathan Garvey didn't want to be resentful, but he felt he couldn't help it. When the inheritance fell through and the Ingallses' farm went to public auction, the tables turned. Jonathan bought his friend's farm for two cents and then gave it back to Charles as a gift. Celebrating has a way of transferring joy to all of us.

A tranquil heart gives life to the flesh, but envy makes the bones rot.

PROVERBS 14:30 ESV

Has envy affected your friendships? Are you able to celebrate when others prosper? How do you move from envy to celebration?

PECULIAR PEOPLE

"Don't ever change, Kezia. It's
the people who are different
who move the mountains."
—REVEREND ALDEN

W hen Kezia moves to Walnut Grove, no one is comfortable with
her. She talks to herself and lives in a home without walls,
and she makes the townspeople nervous. They reject her request for
church membership because she's "too different." Ridiculed for her
strange living arrangement and peculiar way of thinking, she almost
leaves town. Then Reverend Alden reminds the congregation that
unusual people are worth getting to know. Again and again, God
works through unconventional means to bring about miraculous
events.

Jesus was different. He lived an offbeat existence of service and
forgiveness. The Jews were looking for a conquering king, not a
homeless prophet. He spoke boldly, perhaps more boldly than any of
us would be comfortable with.

Kezia and Jesus both said things people didn't like, important
people such as Mrs. Oleson and the Pharisees. Kezia and Jesus were
considered improper, too contrary to the norm. Because of this,
people often rejected the unconditional love they offered.

Investing in people unlocks their true identities. The children of
Walnut Grove got to know Kezia and loved her. The disciples loved

Jesus because they spent time with Him. When we go out of our way to know different people, we might be surprised at the mountain-movers they really are.

> Welcome one another as Christ has welcomed you, for the glory of God.
>
> ROMANS 15:7 ESV

Do you know someone who is different and a bit
intimidating? How can you get to know him or her?

WHEN TREES FALL

"I know how he feels—plowing, planting,
praying for the right weather."
—CHARLES INGALLS

Whether we plow our fields in hopes of a bumper crop or work overtime to get a promotion, at times our plans fail. When Jonathan Garvey's barn burns down with his harvested crops inside, he is crushed. Charles understands how he's feeling, working so hard and coming up empty-handed.

When my kids were young, we moved to a lovely home in the country. It sat on three acres, with a big open field and a chicken coop. After the spring rains, a pond would form with ducks swimming in the shade of two willow trees.

Nearly every summer day, my children spent their afternoons in one of the trees over the dried-up pond. They loved to scoot out to the far end of one mas-

sive limb. Obviously we needed a tree fort. All kinds of ideas came up. Josh invited his dad over to sketch the plans and persuaded him to help with the construction.

Footings, supports, and the floor took shape; the railing and the ladder were in place. One day my father in-law told us the fort was nearly done. Soccer practice kept us away from home that afternoon, so my husband pulled into the driveway before we did. Suddenly he heard the whoosh of tree branches—then stood shaking his head at the destroyed fort.

Sometimes our expectations come crashing down. Time and money are wasted, and a barn full of corn burns. We don't always know why trees fall or fires break out. Is God angry with us?

Disappointment can be hard to bear, especially when there isn't an explanation. Perhaps the Creator of all wants to reveal His absolute power. Maybe seeing His timing and His goodness as gifts are reason enough. I know the tree could have fallen two months earlier, before we cut the first piece of lumber for the fort. I'm fully aware of the opposite as well—my children playing pirates as the tree tumbled with them in it.

Troubles are all around us, their explanations often lacking. God, in His wild pursuit of relationship, presents the opportunity for us to trust. If we can trust Him with crops and tree forts, then how much more can we trust when real trouble comes around?

The LORD is good. He protects those who trust him in times of trouble.

NAHUM 1:7 CEV

Have you ever planned for something only to see
it fail? How did God redirect your best-laid plans,
and what did you learn through the process?

8 o

SOMETHING NEW

*"I've got this feeling. It's like God came down
and gave me back my sight and then said,
'Okay, let's see what you can do.'"*

—Adam Kendall

Our God is an expert in making us new. As we emerge from our more difficult experiences, we can often recognize His plan shining brighter than before. We are motivated to make a difference. After Adam Kendall regains his sight, a new dream fills his heart. He wants to be a lawyer, a vocation he would never have pursued as a blind man. God gives him the determination to try something new.

As I've mentioned, I had the same sensation after brain surgery. For the first time, the world seemed so full of possibilities. I'd never been a writer, unless you count college term papers and thank-you notes. But the overwhelming goodness of God and a life of stories filled my heart. Surviving brain surgery strengthened my faith and my confidence to write.

Resolved health problems have a way of inspiring new endeavors. We dream bigger dreams than before. When we fully realize where we've been and where we are now, our determination skyrockets. God takes someone weak and broken and paves a path toward new seasons of inspiration and hope. People can't help but notice the change.

Adam's dreams come true when he passes the bar exam. His healing from God fuels his passion to succeed as a lawyer. My passion for writing started after my own new beginning. No matter what we've been through, if we stay alert for His leading, God gives each of us the ability to try something new.

> He has given me a new song to sing, a hymn of praise to our God. Many will see what he has done and be amazed. They will put their trust in the LORD.
>
> PSALM 40:3 NLT

What has happened in your life that opened a new door or led you in a new direction? How did it change you?

81

REACH OUT

"When folks stay apart like we have,
you get to feeling like strangers."
—Mr. Tibbs

After our last day on *Little House*, Baby Grace seemed to fall off the Hollywood radar. We watched the show after school every day, but we lost contact with the cast—our *Little House* family. Mr. Tibbs experiences something similar. His children have moved away, and they don't come to visit after his wife dies. It's been so long since he's seen them that Mr. Tibbs fears his family won't know him if he reaches out to them.

Twenty-three years after the NBC good-bye party, we received an invitation to the first *Little House* cast reunion. Walking into the Hollywood Park Race Track, nervous and elephant-sized pregnant, I was welcomed with love from a long-lost family of friends. The cast couldn't believe how grown-up we were. How could Baby Grace possibly be expecting a baby of her own? The day exceeded my expectations; I was part of the *Little House* family again.

It's natural to be hesitant when we reunite with family or friends. We fear it might be awkward or intimidating. Albert and James encourage Mr. Tibbs to contact his children. When we feel distanced from the people we care about, someone has to take the first step. Why not you and me?

Let us not neglect our meeting together, as some people do, but encourage one another, especially now that the day of his return is drawing near.

HEBREWS 10:25 NLT

With whom would you like to reconnect with? What is your first step?

ARTFUL EXPRESSION

*"I can always tell when Pa is sad by the way he plays
the fiddle. It almost sounds like the fiddle is crying."*
—Laura Ingalls

Musicians can speak volumes without uttering a word. The music offers a window to their souls, a clear pane of glass to see what they are feeling. The sound of live music begs us to engage with our emotions. Even children notice joy or sorrow in the melodies of instrumentalists.

When the mill in Walnut Grove closes, Charles Ingalls is left without a job. He can't pay the bill at the mercantile and he feels like a failure. Laura hears her Pa's sadness. The fiddle in his hands can't pretend to be happy. Expressing ourselves through artistic talents is a gift to those around us because we reveal our true feelings.

My daughter loves to draw. She pairs her favorite scenes with fun or insightful quotes. She uses both words and art to express herself. I've noticed that I can determine her internal emotional state by her artwork.

When she is happy, her drawings are filled with flowers and animals. When she is down, her pictures are serious portraits or perhaps a rugged landscape.

We all use different ways to express ourselves. One way is not better than another. It is important to have a healthy outlet to release our joys and disappointments. Pa played the fiddle, my daughter is an artist, and I write stories. Whether we are happy or sad, our artistic abilities communicate what is happening inside. Give the people around you a glimpse of the messages God created you to share with others.

Just as we have many members in one body and all the members do not have the same function, so we, who are many, are one body in Christ, and individually members one of another.

ROMANS 12:4–5 NASB

How do you express yourself artistically? How does your art form voice the emotion within?

83
_____

SHINE BRIGHT

"Since the first day you came through
that door, you lit this whole place
up, like some kind of angel."
—HOUSTON LAMB

S ome people seem to light up a room. No matter what's going on, their attitude and outlook glow like twinkly lights hanging over a back porch. It's a soft radiance, gracefully filling the space. At the school for the blind, irritable handyman Houston sees that glistening light in Mary. Her actions and kindness give him a sense of belonging for the first time in years.

While we may not embody the graceful presence of angels, we can all shine the light of Jesus to those around us. Words of encouragement can turn a life around, and sometimes quietly listening is just as impactful. Every kindness is a stone thrown into a pond—the ripples drifting out make a difference.

I have a friend who is a ray of sunshine to me. The radiance of her spirit is calming, and her words are filled with wisdom. She listens with such intensity, I can't help but share my joys and problems with her.

We can and should seek to shine God's brilliant light. My precious friend shines beautifully like Mary Ingalls. When we live for Jesus, sparks are fanned into a flame of faith for others to see. Love God and shine bright.

"Let your light shine before men in such a way that they may see your good works, and glorify your Father who is in heaven."

MATTHEW 5:16 NASB

Do you know anyone who lights up a room? How can
you shine your light on the people around you?

84

FLEX YOUR MUSCLES

"Sometimes we just have to make people do things whether they like it or not, for their own good."
—Caroline Ingalls

As a parent, I often struggle to make the right decisions for my children. My son and daughter don't always want to invest the time or energy in the activities I believe will benefit them. I'm tempted to let them have the final say just to keep the peace, even though I feel strongly about my point of view. Caroline Ingalls gives her share of advice to her neighbors and friends concerning their children. She reminds us also to flex our parental muscles and listen to our internal voice of wisdom.

A few months ago, my son had to decide on electives for the upcoming school year. We didn't agree on his choices. As I was talking to my mom later that night, she told me a story.

In junior high, she found herself in the same position as my son. She wanted to take ceramics, but her mother insisted on a public speaking class. Speaking had always been a challenge because she stuttered. Nothing my mother said could change my grandmother's mind. Mom was forced to take the class, overcame her impediment, and the *next* semester made beautiful pottery.

My mom told me the speech class was the best she could have taken. Now she speaks in front of people regularly, leads a grief group at her church, and is often the first person to share a memory or story in a large gathering. Her mother wasn't afraid to stand firm on her conviction. The story gave me courage to do the same.

We all need help making the right decisions. Outside of God's Word, our greatest resources are the parents and role models He puts in our lives. We don't always accept their words of wisdom. Even Caroline has to go against a young woman's wishes for her own good. Listening to godly advice will prepare you to share your wisdom with others.

> Good friend, follow your father's good advice; don't wander from your mother's teachings. . . . For sound advice is a beacon, good teaching is a light, moral discipline is a life path.
> PROVERBS 6:20–23 MSG

Has anyone ever persuaded you to do something you didn't want to do? How did it work out? Can your wisdom help someone make a decision?

85

STANDING TALLER INSIDE

*"It doesn't make me feel old, but
it does make me proud."*

—Caroline Ingalls

Children grow up before our eyes. It's been happening since the inception of children. One day you're chasing after a toddler and the next she's asking to borrow your shoes. The moments in between trickle by, one drop at a time, collecting into pools of memories we hope will last forever. We see our children stand tall, and it makes us stand a little taller inside.

Caroline has the same feeling watching Laura prepare for her first teaching job. If she had been focusing on herself she might have felt her age, but instead Ma floats with pride as she looks at the woman her daughter has become.

My children have a few more years before they enter the workforce, but I'm already proud of the people they are becoming. I see kindness and thoughtfulness in them. They know how to work hard, even when the job's lousy and there's no paycheck. I could feel old, but I don't. It is a good thing because these nearly grownup people still require lots of direction and transportation. My job of loving them is far from over.

Children make us proud when we see them moving toward maturity, and regardless of how productive or successful they become, we love them. Even if Laura had failed as a teacher, Caroline's love wouldn't have. When we embrace faith in Jesus, Father God is proud to call us His children. His love for us doesn't depend on our accomplishments, but on the fact that we are His.

> See how very much our Father loves us, for he calls us his children, and that is what we are!
>
> 1 JOHN 3:1 NLT

If you are a parent, what do you see in your children that makes you stand a little taller? In what way was your mother or father proud of you?

86

PEOPLE AREN'T PERFECT

"I think you are only human."
—Caroline Ingalls

W ho doesn't make mistakes from time to time? Our motives are sometimes selfish, and our efforts fail. Expecting perfection in ourselves and others is not realistic. No matter how hard we try, we will stumble. The new banker of Walnut Grove rejects a dinner invitation and accuses Charles of trying to butter him up to get a loan. Pa is discouraged by his own tainted motives, but Caroline reminds him that people aren't perfect.

I married a soccer player. We eat and breathe the sport. My husband coaches and the kids play, which means I watch a lot of soccer. One night Josh came home with a story for the dinner table. He was watching the girls he'd coached as freshmen play their opening game of their senior season. Sitting next to an experienced coaching friend, he caught a nugget of wisdom.

The other team had a breakaway, pretty much a golden opportunity for a goal. The player took a shot and it went wide. The entire sideline groaned. The coaches and parents shook their heads in disbelief.

Josh's friend wasn't disappointed. She sighed and said, "It's really hard to be human." So true, right? We are not perfect and never will be, but the pressure we put on ourselves to perform is paralyzing. We will miss opportunities, make bad decisions, and live with regrets. Caroline Ingalls knows this, and so do we.

The only human who ever reached perfection was Jesus, and He had divinity working for Him. No amount of trying will lead to a life without sin, without error. But grace. . . . Oh, what a gift to receive His grace. To know that when we fail, God can restore us. If we were perfect, we wouldn't need His grace, and we wouldn't need Him.

> Long before he laid down earth's foundations, he had us in mind, had settled on us as the focus of his love, to be made whole and holy by his love.
>
> EPHESIANS 1:4 MSG

How can we give grace to ourselves and others when we stumble? How does imperfection draw us closer to Jesus?

87

TRUE FRIENDS

"We got something here that's just
about the most important thing
in the world—true friends."
—ALICE GARVEY

True friendship multiplies joys and divides sorrows. Friends make new adventures more fun. When the Garvey family makes the difficult decision to move to Winoka, Alice knows having genuine friends like the Ingallses is all she needs to feel at home.

I've been blessed with numerous friends during different stages of my life. My first "tribe" goes back to *Little House.* Being so young, I didn't know the cast members very well then, but our bonds have grown into beautiful friendships.

They have supported me my whole life. Some sent me emails when my children were born. Matt Labyorteaux (Albert Ingalls) reached out with a personal message after my stepdad passed away, and Dean Butler (Almanzo Wilder) helped me with a new business idea. Lindsey Greenbush (Carrie Ingalls) hosted my husband and me in her guest room for a fund-raising event.

While writing this book, I have been amazed at the encouragement from Alison Arngrim (Nellie Oleson) and Karen Grassle (Caroline Ingalls). Charlotte (Miss Beadle), Hersha (Alice Garvey), and Radames (John Jr. Edwards) are dear friends. Every cast trip is a joyous reunion. I'm blessed to be part of the *Little House* family.

God gives us friends to travel with through life. Alice Garvey knows that few things on earth are as valuable as friendship. Find your true friends and treasure them.

Friends come and friends go, but a true friend sticks by you like family.

PROVERBS 18:24 MSG

Who are your true friends? How do you support them?

88

THE BEST, NOT
THE WORST

*"Until we hear different, there's no
point in borrowing trouble."*
—Grace Edwards

Why is it our minds jump to worst-case scenarios? If we haven't heard any news, we assume a situation is bad. When Mary is in the hospital fighting for her life, Laura is home worrying if her sister will survive. Grace Edwards encourages Laura to focus on what is true, reminding Laura that dwelling on potentially negative outcomes doesn't help anyone.

After my brain surgery, tissue was sent to Mayo Clinic Cancer Research Center to be tested. My surgeon wasn't certain if the tumor was cancerous. Ten days of waiting, worry, and dread occupied me. I borrowed trouble that wasn't yet a reality.

Patience is a difficult virtue to master, especially as we wait to receive results concerning our health or the health of a loved one. We have a choice to make: fill our minds with anxiety or with truth. I wish I had chosen better.

The test results eventually revealed a benign tumor. Hallelujah was in order, but the real problem was that I hadn't learned to dwell on truth. The good news is that plenty of chances would present themselves in the near future.

I have lain on a hard platform as it rolls back into the gray dome for a brain scan seven times more since surgery. Seven chances to make a choice. Each time, my mind is filled with memories of my initial diagnosis, and familiar fears flood over me. If I don't stay focused on the truth and the hope I have in Christ, I drown at the possibility of one tiny spot changing everything, again.

My dreams are on hold while I wait for a green light from my doctor each year. And I'm faced with the decision again. It happened not long ago. This time I chose truth. I recited every verse, every beautiful song I could think of. And then I thanked God for being with me through the thumping and the beeping and lying in complete stillness while my thoughts raced wildly. I continued speaking truth to myself as I waited for the phone to ring and for the yes or no from my surgeon.

Our minds—left to themselves—worry. God has given us the ability to train our minds to influence our thoughts. When we fill our minds with God's truth, worry is replaced with trust. Dwelling on the best, not the worst, would have given Laura hope. It's a choice we all have the opportunity to make.

> You'll do best by filling your minds and meditating on things true, noble, reputable, authentic, compelling, gracious—the best, not the worst; the beautiful, not the ugly; things to praise, not things to curse.
>
> PHILIPPIANS 4:8 MSG

Have you ever waited for life-altering results?
Did you choose worry or truth? How can you
begin to fill your mind with God's truth?

LIVING WITH PURPOSE

"I was put here on this planet for a purpose,
maybe not an exalted purpose, but a purpose."
—Annabelle Oleson

E very person on planet Earth has a purpose. God created us to glorify Him and enjoy His presence. But God's calling for each of us is different. He invites us to live out our unique set of gifts to accomplish His mission. Annabelle, the Fat Lady of the traveling circus, found her calling in making people

happy with laughter. She knew her purpose might not seem noble, but bringing smiles to people's faces gave her life meaning.

I haven't always known God's calling for me. At times my actions and words have felt meaningless, my time and effort wasted. No matter how hard I tried to conjure up significance, I fell short. Blazing our own trail can lead to bad directions and dead ends. But God creates a paved detour back to His plan for us.

Playing the role of Baby Grace has been with me for more than forty years. I always imagined God orchestrating it for a greater purpose than simply a paycheck. People who love *Little House* love the character of Baby Grace. The silly faces and cries of a baby on television have given me the opportunity to share the story of God's goodness and grace. Every time I speak to fans, my goal is to make God famous, not myself. That's my purpose.

Living without purpose can be an empty existence. Often we fall into the trap of believing we are useless, especially to God. As Annabelle discovered, nothing could be further from the truth. God wants all of us to join Him on the adventure of a lifetime. He will use every willing heart and every quirky personality to make His name known.

> "I have spared you for a purpose—to show you my power and to spread my fame throughout the earth."
> EXODUS 9:16 NLT

Have you ever tried to create your own purpose? What happened? What are the unique abilities or opportunities God has blessed you with?

90

EVEN IF

"If He doesn't, will you lose your faith?"
—OLD MAN

W hen we pray for a miracle, we have to ask ourselves if our faith will remain even if the miracle doesn't come. Or will it fall apart, as if we were trusting the miracle rather than the God of miracles?

God has the power to heal us and our loved ones, but how we respond says everything about surrender. When Charles Ingalls's son James is shot and lies in a coma, Charles goes into the woods to pray and build an altar to God. An angel, whom he names Old Man, asks him the question. Charles's response is a confident no. Nothing can take away his faith in God.

Whatever happens, it doesn't change who God is. If He doesn't move the mountains or raise the dead, He's still faithful. He's still good.

A small piece of metal stamped with IT IS WELL hangs on a chain around my neck. I made it after my surgery, and I rarely take it off. It reminds me that *even if* God doesn't do what I hope or ask, He has been faithful to me through so much, I'm not about to give up on Him now. "It Is Well" is more than a song or saying. It is total surrender to Jesus, our Lord and King.

The Ingalls family had their share of joys and sorrows, just as we do. Charles demonstrates to his family (and a world of viewers) that

God is worth trusting. Even in the hardest moments of life, even if He doesn't answer our prayers. Even if the events of your life are leaving you hopeless and you don't think you can go on another day, God is with you, He is trustworthy, and He loves you. Hold fast to your faith.

> If we are thrown into the blazing furnace, the God whom we serve is able to save us. . . . But even if he doesn't, we want to make it clear to you, Your Majesty, that we will never serve your gods.
>
> DANIEL 3:17–18 NLT

What happens when your prayers seem to go unanswered? Is God still good even if He doesn't answer the way you had hoped?

9 I

TELL YOUR STORY

"They're not real, honey; they're just stories."
—CAROLINE INGALLS

O ur lives are made up of stories—good and bad. Few are neutral. Stories can frighten us, encourage us, explain or question, make us laugh or bring us to tears. Some stories are truth as best as we can remember it, and others are pretend. Even pretend stories fall into more than one category—entertaining, silly, or laced with life lessons. Carrie wants Ma to believe in fairy tales and larger-than-life strawberries. Caroline, a no-nonsense grown-up, tells her daughter she doesn't have time for such things. All the wishing in the world can't change Ma's mind.

As a child, I never thought my stories mattered. I lived life tucking away my personal experiences, never sharing them. The first time someone asked me to share the story of my faith, a chill rushed through me. *Why would anyone want to hear my story?*

I definitely had segments of memories and experiences, but the resolution was missing. I couldn't see the good that strung the pieces together. I hadn't discovered what purpose God had for what I'd been through. Sometimes it takes more time than we'd like for our stories to take shape.

Two weeks after my surgery, I started to see the beginnings of connecting points. God gave me a voice I never thought I possessed. When I shared my story at a youth conference, God gave me courage to articulate where I'd been and what He was doing in my life.

Since that day, stories are swimming around in my head. Stories inspire, challenge, and connect us with others. Every little story we share is a piece of His much bigger story. Jesus is the Hero who rescues, protects, and supplies. He gives hope, and joy, and peace. When I tell about my adventures, I hope others are encouraged to share theirs too.

God is the ultimate Storyteller, orchestrating our lives into a collection of unforgettable tales. Every person has a story to share, and every story has the power to change a life. Your stories reveal the testimony of God's hand on you. Only you can tell your story.

I'm not one to disagree with Ma, but our stories are never *just* stories.

Let the redeemed of the LORD tell their story—those he redeemed from the hand of the foe, those he gathered from the lands, from the east and west, from north and south.

PSALM 107:2–3 NIV

Do you think your stories matter? Whom do you share your stories with? How can you give God glory through your testimony?

ACKNOWLEDGMENTS

First, all glory and thanks go to Jesus—the One who has written every story on the pages of my life, transforming even my hardest moments into something beautiful so I could share His hope with you.

This project wouldn't have taken flight without Trip Friendly. Trip's late father, Ed Friendly, first acquired the rights to *Little House on the Prairie*, cocreating and coproducing the show. Trip's tremendous support and permission to use quotes from the television series *Little House on the Prairie* has made this book possible. Thank you with all my heart.

Thank you to MacKenzie Howard at HarperCollins Publishers for taking a chance on me. Our meeting at Mount Hermon was not an accident, and I am grateful for the way you have walked with me in publishing my first book.

For the entire team at Thomas Nelson, you are all fabulous. I never thought the publishing process could be easy, but it has been a dream. Thank you for all your hard work.

Thank you to my illustrator, Steven Noble—the cover and artwork are more than I ever hoped they would be.

For Cynthia Ruchti, my literary agent: you stepped in at the perfect moment, when I was overwhelmed and needed your expertise. Your time and effort on my manuscript will not be forgotten. Thank you.

I want to thank my writer's group—Ann, Cheryl, Holly, and Rosie. You have seen my worst writing and every time encouraged me to keep working, keep improving my craft. We started out as fellow writers, but now we are friends.

A huge thanks to my prayer team, your prayers have propelled me to shift my perspective and give God the glory above all else. Every one of you is a precious treasure.

For the cast of *Little House*—you are my friends and my family, a special thank you to Alison Arngrim (Nellie Oleson) for supporting me in this project and daring me to dream big.

For all my friends, but especially Jodi, Sarah, and Trenda, you have been with me through very happy and sad times. Thank you for loving me, crying with me, and drinking lots of coffee with me.

For my sisters, Michelle, Brenda, and Heidi, you three have been with me from the beginning. Many of these stories are about all of us. Thank you for allowing me to share them with the world.

For my twin—Brenda, you were Baby Grace too, and without you this book would never have been written. Without you, I would be only a sliver of who I am today.

For my mom, Jackie, thank you for following your heart and sacrificing for us to be on *Little House*. Thank you for raising us to be strong women who love the Lord. I'm forever grateful for your endurance of my endless questions about every *Little House* memory. This book would not be as vivid without your input.

And finally my three loves on this earth—Josh, Tobey, and Raegan. Josh, thank you for letting me chase my dreams and for my nightly backrubs. Tobey, thank you for your dedication in rewatching hundreds of *Little House* episodes with me. And Raegan, thank you for the encouraging words that keep me writing every single day. You three have brought love, joy, and endless snuggles to my life. I love you.

9 781400 247257